Going Viral

Karine Nahon and
Jeff Hemsley

polity

First published in 2013 by Polity Press
Reprinted 2014, 2015, 2016

Polity Press
65 Bridge Street
Cambridge CB2 1UR, UK

Polity Press
350 Main Street
Malden, MA 02148, USA

ISBN-13: 978-0-7456-7128-4
ISBN-13: 978-0-7456-7129-1(pb)

A catalogue record for this book is available from the British Library.

Typeset in 11 on 14 pt Sabon by
Servis Filmsetting Ltd, Stockport, Cheshire
Printed and bound in the United States of America by RR Donnelley

The publisher has used its best endeavours to ensure that the URLs for external websites referred to in this book are correct and active at the time of going to press. However, the publisher has no responsibility for the websites and can make no guarantee that a site will remain live or that the content is or will remain appropriate.

Every effort has been made to trace all copyright holders, but if any have been inadvertently overlooked the publisher will be pleased to include any necessary credits in any subsequent reprint or edition.

For further information on Polity, visit our website: www.politybooks.com

Going Viral

To all of those dedicated to an open Internet

Contents

Figures and Tables

Tables

Acknowledgments

There is so much more to a book than just the writing of it. As such, we are indebted to a large number of people, who answered our questions, shared their data with us, provided some of the graphics for the book, debated with us, and helped us crystalize ideas and concepts or just contributed their time. A special thanks to Gilad Lotan of SocialFlow, who provided us data and graphics related to the viral spread of the news of Osama bin Laden's death and the video of KONY2012; Miguel Rios from Twitter allowed us to use his graphic of Twitter volume regarding Osama bin Laden's death; Simon Rogers of the *Guardian* and Alon Halevi at Google assisted us with the WikiLeaks case; Daphne Koller answered our questions about Coursera; Sarah Wachter graciously allowed us to analyze her YouTube referral data of "Librarians Do Gaga" and Jacques Hebert at MotherJones blog also shared data with us regarding the video of Mitt Romney talking about 47 percent of Americans; Tal Gallili answered questions and shared data related the R-Bloggers website; and

Acknowledgments

Alex Constant helped us gather and interpret materials about the Rosa Parks case. Elliott Karstadt, Jennifer Jahn, and Neil de Cort at Polity Press worked behind the scenes on *Going Viral* and guided us through the publishing process. Arlene Pritzker, Elia Finkelstein, and Melody Lutz all assisted with language edits and feedback, and the anonymous readers provided thoughtful feedback that greatly improved the quality of the text. We thank all of you.

Another category of people who deserve our heartfelt thanks are members of our research teams, colleagues, and mentors whose efforts and input made this work possible. From the retroV research team (supported by a Google Research Award) we thank Muzammil Hussain, Chris Wells, Lance Bennett, and particularly Shawn Walker, whose legendary skill with collecting and stitching together complex data sets are at the heart of a growing list of research projects. Thank you to our colleagues at the Social Media Lab (SoMe Lab, funded by the National Science Foundation), made up of Robert Mason (the Million Dollar Man), Josef Eckert (GeoJoe), and again Shawn Walker (Data Daddy), for their patience, support, input, and assistance, as well as their work on the SoMe Tools project, out of which came the data used in the UC Davis pepper spray case. Further, Jeff thanks Robert Mason for support and guidance, Kirsten Foot for hard questions, and Malcolm Parks for giving virality a chance. Karine thanks Manuel Castells and the members of the working group at the Library of Congress, where the seed for this book was planted, and both of us extend our gratitude to John Thompson for his insistence that we nurture that seed and patience in walking us through the process of writing a book.

Finally, and most importantly, we thank our spouses, Arlene and Michael, Karine's kids (Daniel and Ari) and mother (Ody) for encouraging, understanding, supporting, and enduring our esoteric rants on the topic of virality.

Preface

The idea for this book came about while I was visiting the Library of Congress (LOC) in Washington, DC. For me, LOC is one of the temples of culture of societies. I came to Washington on the invitation of my colleague and friend Manuel Castells, who was participating in a one-week working group about the role of the Library of Congress over the next 25 years. The growing use of social media and the explosion of user-generated content create new challenges and opportunities for libraries. One of the most pressing questions for libraries is what should libraries attempt to collect and curate in this new media environment, given the ease of creating and sharing content, the tremendous and growing volume of this content, as well as the infeasibility of libraries collecting and saving it all. This is where virality comes in. While there, I gave a talk about virality and its impact on society.

My colleagues and I from the retroV research group at the University of Washington's Information School had been researching virality extensively for four years, particularly what it means for society. In the meeting at LOC, I argued that viral information is one indicator of what is important to a particular society at a particular moment. I suggested that as libraries struggle to decide what to curate, a good starting point would be to consider information items that have gone viral. This is because viral events arise out of the complex interactions of many actors – individuals, companies, governments – as well as the social and cultural contexts within which they are embedded. Virality can signal what is considered important and interesting to parts of a society at a particular time, and traces of viral content may also become a way of documenting the fabric of societies. As such, future generations may find the viral events of today valuable lenses into our time, providing insights that we ourselves will miss because of our own embeddedness in the world from which these viral events arise.

Social media makes it very easy to digitally express ourselves and share that expression instantly. It enables some social activity to happen faster and reach farther out into the networks that connect us all. Part of what makes this social infrastructure so interesting is that it is made up of vast interconnected crowds all doing their own thing. Except, sometimes they come together. Sometimes the crowd finds some bit of content remarkable. In fact, they find it so remarkable that within a few days they remark on it, and share it will all of their friends and followers. In a way, a viral event is the collective voice of the crowd saying "this is important!" Whether it's a middle-aged Scottish vocalist who makes us challenge our stereotypes, a humorous protest video that creates a public relations nightmare for a major airline, or an uplifting news story of a flash mob where musicians played the Beatles' tune "Here Comes the Sun" in a busy Spanish unemployment office, viral events are the remarkable bits of culture that rise to the top. Once there, they can quickly focus the public's attention on police brutality against peaceful protestors, the personal infidelity of high-ranking officials, or the suffering of communities after natural disasters.

After my talk, John Thompson, the editor of Polity Press and one of the working group participants, insisted that I write a book, arguing that our knowledge of virality should be available to the public at large. "A short book," he said, "it shouldn't take long, and yes . . . there is another condition, you need to be ready in four months so it can be published in September the next year." This was July and I had just started my sabbatical. I was resistant because I had planned to write a book about Network Gatekeeping Theory, an area I have been developing over the last ten years.

About a month later I received a persuasive email from John, emphasizing the importance of a book about virality as a bridge between different fields and audiences, all of whom are embedded in this new social media environment and affected by viral events. As he saw it, a book about viral events filled an important niche at the intersection of sociology, information science, communications, political science, and network theory. I already knew that most books about virality discussed it from within a particular academic lens, from a popular point of view, or from a marketing perspective, so I agreed.

Now that I was on board, I was left with questions. What's the best way to tell the story using the integrated lenses of social and exact science? How does one bring the story and knowledge about virality to both a general and academic audience at the same time? Finally, as I have mentioned, one of my key interests over the past decade has been about gatekeepers, actors who, through their own discretion, control information flows. As I saw it, gatekeepers played such a critical role in viral events that I could certainly write a book just about their role. But, the book also needed to be balanced by talking about people, their role in driving these processes, the crowd, social media, and the networks that connect us all. Also, a fair amount of literature discusses the technical aspects of how information flows in networks, and, while John and I did not want to create a technical book, I knew the arguments needed to be backed up by rigorous, qualitative, and quantitative empirical research.

At this point I contacted my PhD student, Jeff Hemsley. For the past few years he has been immersed in the study of virality. His perspective was more quantitative and bottom-up. I knew that his expertise would balance my top-down research and studies of virality. He saw network structures, crowds, and the emerging social infrastructure as being primary drivers for viral events. Having worked with him on other projects in our research groups, I knew that he would be the perfect person to bring these needed perspectives. Together we decided to take up the challenge and try to tell the story from both the top-down and the bottom-up perspectives. Interestingly enough, even though we have been researching virality together for a few years, we were surprised at just how far apart our views were. The journey has been full of arguments, debates, agreements, persuasions, and compromises.

We have found that the process of argumentation has helped us to crystalize our thoughts as we strive for accuracy and rigorousness. It has led to moments of epiphany and new insights, but also to frustration and compromise when we find that sometimes there is no perfect word; that any word may be laden with alternate meanings.

How much of virality is controllable? To what extent is it predictable? Is it a process that can be designed or does it emerge out of the whims of the crowd? What are the roles of network and social structures? These are some of the questions that, at the start, we were deeply opposed about. Sometimes, writing a book with a partner is not an easy task, but it has its advantages. Through our discussions, we have both arrived at a "center point," one that we hope will open the door to future studies on the topic. Yes, there are still a few things we disagree about, but the rewarding part of partnership is growth and understanding. I have probably learned as much from my PhD student as he has from me, and that is how it should be.

At the outset, we knew that if we created a cookbook of how to create viral events, it could sell many copies to marketers and practitioners, but our scientific truth was different. The audience we hope to reach is our own scientific community, but we also think that understanding how viral events work, how they impact society, and their value to future generations can better prepare people to operate in the emerging social infrastructure. As such, we have tried to make this book as readable as possible in the hope that each one of you can gain insight into the events that we call viral events.

Karine Nahon
Tel-Aviv
March 2013

Cover Art

"Occupying Twitter: A retweet network." Jeff created this visualization from Twitter data captured during the days leading up to, and just after, the Occupy Oakland protesters shut down the Oakland ports on November 2, 2011. Each dot is a Twitter user and each line is a case where one user retweeted another user. The large clusters of dots typically represent viral events about the port shut down or other news related to Occupy Oakland. The disconnected clusters at the lower part of the image represent large retweet events, some viral, by people not necessarily connected to the protesters, but who otherwise are tweeting about Occupy Oakland – sometimes in harsh terms. The data was drawn from the Social Media Lab's corpus of Occupy Tweets.

1

Introduction: Virality of pets and presidents

Viral information is not new. When we look back in time, before the Internet, there are plenty of examples of fast-moving information flows that reached many people and happened as a result of people sharing – the key elements of virality. One likely candidate is the news of the arrest of Rosa Parks, on Thursday, December 1, 1955. She was arrested in Montgomery, Alabama, for not giving up her seat to a white person on a segregated bus (Parks and Haskins 1999). Instead of the Internet, people used phones, hand-bills, and word of mouth. It is estimated that within three days, roughly 40,000 blacks had heard about, and joined a boycott of the bus system in protest at Rosa Park's arrest (Dove 1999). They walked, often miles, every day to their schools and jobs. And they continued to walk for more than a year until the segregation law was repealed.

Viral events are not new. What *is* new is that a viral video, a news story, or a photo can reach 40,000 people in hours, or even minutes, instead of days. And it isn't just the speed and reach of these information flows that makes them worth understanding; it is their frequency. We would be hard pressed to find more than a handful of viral events from the 1950s, but today viral events are ubiquitous. Viral events are a naturally occurring, emergent phenomenon facilitated by the interwoven collection of websites that allow users to host and share content (YouTube, Instagram, Flickr), connect with friends and people with similar interests (Facebook, Twitter), and share their knowledge (Wikipedia, blogs). Collectively, these sites have formed a social infrastructure that we refer to as social media. In this new information ecosystem, an individual can share information that can flash across our digitally supported social networks with a speed and reach never before available to the vast majority of people. It can go viral.

Of course, even in their ubiquity viral events are the exception while the vast majority of content remains obscure. Viral content is what stands out as *remarkable* in a sea of content. What do we mean when we claim that something has *gone viral*? And what is virality's impact on society? In this book we explore these and many other questions about the nature of viral events facilitated by our new social infrastructure. To do this we will use examples of well-known viral videos, tweets, and news stories that spread so fast that we, as researchers, pundits, journalists, and individuals, wrote about just exactly that: how far and how fast the video, tweet, or story spread. We will also draw on digital content that spread virally within interest communities.

Before looking at our first few viral cases, we need to address the first, and perhaps most important, question about virality: why should you invest your attention, an increasingly scarce resource, reading about virality? And, perhaps more importantly, why *this* book? Unlike many pundits and researchers, we don't think virality is an absolute game-changer that empowers the masses. We also don't think it is yet another control mechanism of the political, media, and financial elites. Instead, we will argue that virality can both reproduce and transform existing social norms and institutions. To do so we will explore how virality works by looking at real-life examples, our own research, and the research of many others who are seeking to understand how information flows in social media. We will show that virality is a complex process and provide a theoretical model that will be useful in understanding how virality works and the effects it can have on individuals, collectives, and institutions, and that it feeds back into and affects social systems. This approach requires that we synthesize two, often completing, perspectives; first, a technical, quantitative perspective that helps us explain network structures and gives us ways to identify, describe, and visualize viral events; and second, a more qualitative social perspective, wherein we examine the qualities of specific viral events and draw on well-known existing social theories to describe virality as a social process and outline its effects in our current and future societies.

Virality's prevalence in contemporary society is an emergent feature of the interconnected social media platforms that together have created a dynamic *social infrastructure*. In other words, for better or worse, we think virality is here to stay and that those who can ride its wave will enjoy a competitive advantage in whatever sea of human attention – big or small – they surf in.

Our first example involves a singer and a savvy producer. Before her audition on the TV show *Britain's Got Talent*, no one would have predicted that Susan Boyle could reach an audience of close to 100 million people in less than ten days. But that is what happened. Within just a few days of being posted, almost 2 million people watched the YouTube video[1] of Ms. Boyle singing "I Dreamed a Dream" from *Les Misérables* on *Britain's Got Talent*.

Susan Boyle didn't fit the bill of a global singing sensation. She wasn't young and trim, the piece she selected for her audition on *Britain's Got Talent* wasn't hip, fresh music, and no one would characterize her presence on stage as commanding. No, the 47-year-old, unemployed, single woman with a cat named Pebbles would better be described as awkward, stout, and frumpy. And yet, as her video gained views on YouTube, interview requests poured in from well-known media outlets such as the *Guardian* newspaper and Reuters. Blogs, from the mighty Huffington Post to a plethora of blogs with only a few followers, posted reactions to the video itself, to Ms. Boyle, and to the phenomenal speed at which the video had reached a global audience.

Speed and reach are nearly always cited as qualities of virality, but how fast and how far does something have to spread for it to be called viral? Where does the concept of virality end and other concepts, such as memes, behavior cascades, and word-of-mouth, start? In chapter 2 we will offer a definition that addresses these and other questions, and support it with a great deal of research, our own as well as many other scholars'. In this chapter we will move toward that definition by identifying specific aspects of virality, starting by agreeing that speed and reach are definitely key elements.

Another idea we tend to think of when we think of virality is that it is simply the result of people sharing amateur content with each other. If that is true, then we have to ask: was the YouTube video of Ms. Boyle singing "I Dreamed a Dream" really an example of a viral video? It was professionally produced with a well-crafted narrative and her voice was apparently auto-tuned,[2] a computerized method of enhancing vocals. Before the video was posted on YouTube, her audition was aired on ITV, a commercial TV network in the United Kingdom. Additionally, a great many prominent news services discussed the video as it gained popularity, which likely caused more people to see it than would have otherwise been the case. On the other hand, Letty Cottin Pogrebin, a prominent Huffington Post blogger, wrote of the video that she "sent the YouTube link to everyone on my Women's Issues list"[3] in what we have come to think of as a typical viral spread: one where each person who sends a link out, sends it to many others, each of whom might again send it to many others so that each time the link is forwarded an ever-increasing audience is exposed to the video, often in a very short time frame.

The case of Susan Boyle is one case among many that exemplifies how fast and far information can spread through networks, and it highlights one of the most important questions about virality: is the viral process driven organically by those who view and spread content; in other words is it a bottom-up process? If not, then is virality something that can be designed by content makers and promoted by powerful gatekeepers, in other words, a top-down process? We address these questions later by exploring the top-down perspective in chapter 3 and the bottom-up perspective in chapter 4. In chapter 5 we tie both perspectives together by showing how both perspectives are subject to structural elements of the networks in which we are all embedded.

In terms of the impact of viral events, Susan Boyle's audition video certainly shows that it can quickly and often unexpectedly propel someone to stardom. Boyle went from singing in her church to performing world tours and reportedly has personal assets worth over £20 million. She is living the dream of many: she is a world-famous, professional musician. Certainly, she would have gained greater attention, and likely more oppor-tunities to perform, just from having been on *Britain's Got Talent*. Virality amplified the affect by bringing Susan to the attention of many people who would oth-erwise not have heard of her. In chapter 4 we delve into some of the reasons why people share content. We also explore the ways we are connected to each other and how that facilitates viral events.

Of course, virality can bring individuals' attention in ways they had not expected. Soon after Alexandra Wallace, a student at the University of Los Angeles, uploaded a racist rant video titled "Asians at the Library,"[4] she suddenly became the focus of a great deal of attention. According to LA Weekly blogger Simone Wilson (Wilson 2011), tens of thousands of people on Facebook had shared the video. Response videos and remixes were showing up on YouTube as well. The video received enough attention that, on the next day, the Huffington Post,[5] one of the most highly visible blogs on the Internet, had learned about the video and reported on it. By Wednesday she was receiving email death threats. She had taken down the video by then, but enough people had copied and reposted the content that it was easily found and reshared again. By March 21, Wallace had publicly apologized and decided to leave UCLA (O'Neil 2011).

Alexandra Wallace wasn't famous to start with, so the question arises, how did people find out about the video? Was it just the result of people sharing the video, one to the next and on and on? Certainly, one fundamental aspect of viral events is that they emerge through people sharing content with other people. However, for content to reach truly large audiences, networks need to be connected, and this is where gatekeepers come in. Gatekeepers are people, collectives, companies, or governments that, as a result of their location in a network, can promote or suppress the movement of information from one part of a network to another. Their role in the flow of information, including viral events, is important enough that we devote most of chapter 3 to them. For now, let's take a quick look at an example of how modern social and communication infrastructures allow people to circumvent the control that gatekeepers normally have over information flows and how people can unexpectedly become gatekeepers on their own.

Just after midnight, on May 2, 2011, two low-flying U.S. Black Hawk helicopters entered Pakistani airspace carrying U.S. Navy Seals. Perhaps the first announcement of this event came from an IT consultant named Sohaib Athar, who tweeted that the presence of the low-flying craft in Abbottabad at such a late hour was a rare and possibly ominous event.[6] Like all but a handful of top-level U.S. officials and C.I.A. operatives, Sohaib could not have guessed the nature of the operation. In the White House Situation Room, President Obama, Vice-President Biden, Secretary of State Clinton and others watched the raid on Osama bin Laden's compound in real time on night-vision screens.[7]

The mission turned out to be successful, but President Obama wanted to wait to make the announcement until DNA testing could confirm that the body was indeed that of Osama bin Laden. His advisers, however, urged him to schedule a briefing, arguing that the story would get out anyway. They were right. And from a source they wouldn't have predicted. Just 38 minutes after the announcement that Obama would address the media, Keith Urbahn, the chief of staff of Donald Rumsfeld, former U.S. Secretary of Defense, tweeted "So I'm told by a reputable person they have killed Osama bin Laden. Hot Damn."[8] His tweet went viral. It was retweeted and talked about by millions before any media outlet or the White House's scheduled press conference could break the news.

The question of who posted content first and the order of those who forwarded this have tremendous importance to the topic of virality. By tracing when people post and share content, we can analyze the life cycle of a viral event and detect important gatekeepers in the process. In chapter 3 we will do so by decomposing the process and studying people and organizations involved in disseminating the information. Not many people followed Keith Urbahn at the time, but one of his followers was the *New York Times* journalist Brian Stelter, who retweeted (shared) Keith's message to his own network.[9] What happened at this point? How did Brian Stelter's tweet affect the trajectory of the viral event?

At the heart of virality lay both the ability and the *decision* of people and organizations to share information. This means that each time we are faced with a decision to forward information into our own networks, we are acting as gatekeepers. In our roles as gatekeepers we can also act as a bridge, connecting disparate networks by allowing information to flow. Herein lay the challenge to many traditional institutions. Instead of CNN or Fox breaking the news of bin Laden's death on TV, Urbahn broke it on Twitter.

In chapter 3 we will look at other examples of viral events that circumvented gatekeepers. What is important here is that virality has the power to challenge institutions precisely because it circumvents gatekeepers and captures public attention. Virality can raise awareness on a given topic, can show new ways of viewing the world, and can expose truths. Virality can transform attitudes and spark intentions to act in new ways. People witnessed this in 2011 as social movements around the world (democratic and non-democratic) emerged to protest against their governments: The Indignant Movement in Spain or Greece, the Tent Movement in Israel, the Occupy Movement in the U.S., or the Arab Spring. We are not claiming that virality caused these events. Far from it. The seeds for each of these events lie in preexisting grievances. But viral events have the potential to get the word out about injustices.

For example, on November 18, 2011, Occupy protesters at the University of California Davis (hereafter:
UC Davis) sat in a line, arms linked, blocking traffic.
As they would not budge, Lieutenant John Pike walked
along the line of protestors and sprayed each one in the
face with pepper spray. Unfortunately for him, many
people in the crowd had cameras. Within seconds,
photos of what appeared to be a cold and callous Pike
spread via social networks and soon after on traditional media as well. The uproar from the public was
focused on Pike, but the university came under fire as
well. A heated discourse developed around the photo
on blogs, Twitter and Facebook. The most significant
refrain demanded accountability for Lieutenant Pike's
actions. The public needed to make sense of the event
and understand how Pike could do such a thing, and
how the university could allow it. One outcome was
that the board of UC Davis issued a statement calling
for the resignation of the Chancellor of the university
and the end of police policies of removing non-violent
demonstrators from the campus. As for Lieutenant John
Pike, as of August 2012 he is no longer employed by
the university. We have no doubt that the viral spread
of the photos and videos played a critical role in forcing the institution of the university to be accountable
for their actions. Accountability is only one element in
a bigger story of how virality helps in promoting the
principles of open government: transparency, accountability, and participation of the public. We will discuss
this in depth in chapter 5 and 6.

It is worth noting that many people took pictures and
movies of Pike's actions. Certainly most of these photos

and videos did not go viral, but enough did to create a climate that forced the university to act. In many of the examples we will use in this book, we will focus on a single viral event: a tweet, a video, a photo, a news story, or a computer game. The UC Davis case is an example of many viral and non-viral events that, together, formed a *trending*, or *viral, topic*. In a viral topic, many posts and shares interact and feed off of each other in a digitally mediated conversation. Some of these posts and shares are viral events in their own right and contribute to and shape the larger topic. Viral topics share similar features with individual viral events, and we will explore this in more detail later because understanding how individual viral events and viral topics are similar and different will be an important part of understanding how virality both transforms and recreates our society. For now, let's zoom back in to the scale of a single viral event to help us understand how one viral video created tremendous negative publicity for United Airlines.

While waiting to deplane a United Airlines flight at Chicago O'Hare International Airport, David Carroll, his band, and other passengers saw baggage handlers out on the tarmac tossing guitars to each other while removing luggage from the plane. When he collected his checked luggage at his final destination, he discovered that the neck of his $3,500 Taylor guitar had been broken. According to Carroll, United's customer service responded with complete indifference to his plight, and he spent the next nine months seeking compensation from United.

When Carroll and his band "Sons of Maxwell" posted a YouTube video titled "United Breaks Guitars,"[10] it resonated with people. As bloggers posted links to the video they received comments like, "It's musical, it's funny, it wears well, and it really hits a raw spot,"[11] ". . . think back to the last time an airline lost your luggage, or damaged it, or just plain didn't care,"[12] and "I just flew United and when I got home found that someone had stolen 6 bottles of wine out of a 12 bottle case I had checked. Now I'm getting the runaround. United blows!!"[13]

We can quickly see one reason why viral videos like "United Breaks Guitars" matter to organizations with some very simple math.[14] The video is 4 minutes and 37 seconds long and by Monday, July 20, 2009, it had been viewed about 3.5 million times. That is 16 million minutes of negative, but funny, advertising within just two weeks. In his book, *The Black Swan: The Impact of the Highly Improbable*, Taleb suggests that the events we believe will never happen – the most highly improbable ones – are often the ones that, once they do happen, change everything (2010). The "United Breaks Guitars" video was a black swan event. We make this claim because for a company like United, it could never happen that one disgruntled customer could suddenly cause so much bad publicity. But it did happen. And it changed the business environment by making companies aware that abusing their hyperconnected customers could come at a high price indeed. Enough so that the *Harvard Business Review*, a respected journal in the business world, has done a careful analysis of the event so other companies are aware of the possibilities (2012). In chapter 2, we use this case again as it will help us define virality, and then again in chapter 4 as we explore some of the reasons why people forward messages. For now, we will use this example to talk more about how the element of viral speed works.

If you are the original poster of a YouTube video, you can download the referral data to get a clear picture of the number of times the video was viewed in a single day, as well as what sites people watched the video on or came to YouTube from. Without access to that data, you can still get a fairly good picture by finding blogs that mentioned how many views the video already had at the time the blogger linked to it. Using this method we know that the first view count mention was on July 7: 320. By late in the day, the view count had grown to 3,500, and the highest view count noted for the July 8, 9, and 10 were 200,000, 500,000 and 1.5 million, respectively. By the July 14, bloggers report that the video had around 3 million views, after which it took another six days to get to 3.5 million. If we plotted these numbers on a graph, we would see a slow climb on the first day or two, then a very steep growth in the view count, followed by a leveling off. This sort of slow-fast-slow growth is typical of viral events and happens for a number of reasons that we will discuss further in chapter 2.

The important take-away for now is that for a video or a tweet or a news story, or whatever, to be viral it must be spread by people to other people, and that we can, in many cases, verify that something is viral by looking for the slow-fast-slow signature. In chapter 4, we will use this video and others to explain how the ways in which people are connected affects how information flows.

As authors, our goal in this book is to explore the concept of virality in depth and to make its interworkings more transparent, accessible, and understandable to a broad audience. Whether you are a scholar, a politician, a policy maker, an executive, a marketer, an artist, or an activist, we hope this book will be useful as you navigate our emerging media ecosystem. As scholars, we hope that this work will contribute to the growing discussion aimed at helping society better understand how virality and other types of information flows are shaped by and shape the world we live in.

2

What Virality Is: I know it when I see it

Viral information can transform society by changing people's awareness, norms, and behaviors around events and issues. In our contemporary society we hear quite often about videos or tweets *going viral*, but virality is just one type of information flow. Information can spread to people through different channels, at different speeds. Information can be broadcasted to mass audiences, or shared on small and large scales; it can be spread when people talk around the water cooler, or one-on-one in whispers, like a rumor. The *way* information spreads, the context and structures it is embedded in, have an effect on whether or not people pay attention to it and how influential that information is. Two of the key things we hope to communicate with this book are, first, that virality is a specific type of information flow and, second, that because of the process by which it flows, it is influential both at the individual and societal level. Our focus in this chapter is to address the first part of that statement by defining what virality is and differentiating it from other types of information flows (i.e., non-viral or popular information, memes, cascades, and word-of-mouth).

When is a video a *viral* video as opposed to a popular or an obscure one? Is it the number of views? If it is, would the video "Librarians Do Gaga,"[1] which got 250,000 views before it peaked, be considered viral, or do you need to have at least a few million views like Carroll's "United Breaks Guitars"? What about how fast it reaches its audience? The "United Breaks Guitars" video reached 1.5 million people in four days, but a math tutor video from the Kahn Academy has been viewed 1.3 million times[2] at a fairly steady rate over two years. Are both of these examples viral? Finally, how far does information need to spread to be considered viral? The purpose of this chapter is to provide a clear definition of virality so we can avoid falling back on "I know it when I see it."

Virality is a social information flow process where many people simultaneously forward a specific information item, over a short period of time, within their social networks, and where the message spreads beyond their own [social] networks to different, often distant networks, resulting in a sharp acceleration[3] in the number of people who are exposed to the message.[4] Therefore, identifying and measuring virality is made on the bases of (i) the human and social aspects of information sharing from one to another; (ii) the speed of spread; (iii) the reach in terms of the number of people exposed to the content; and (iv) the reach in terms of the distance the information travels by bridging multiple networks. In this chapter we elaborate on each of these elements, but first, we will briefly look at how the meaning of viral events or virality has changed over time and note why a clear definition is useful.

Just a few decades ago, people would assume that the meaning of the phrase "viral event" would have something to do with biological viruses and diseases. Words come into, and are retired from, our daily vocabulary all the time. Even their meaning and use change over time. So is the case with "virality." Our current use of the term is derived from its origins in biology, but was adopted by the field of marketing, which should come as no surprise as information and viruses have some commonalities. Both rely on carriers and can mutate while spreading, but "While viruses tend to be indiscriminate, infecting any susceptible individual, information is selective" (Huberman and Adamic 2004).

The field of marketing has been abuzz with the terms "viral" or "viral marketing" or "viral word-of-mouth" since 1997, when Jurvetson coined the term "viral marketing" after witnessing how the free email product HotMail spread from user to user in a "pattern of rapid adoption through word-of-mouth networks" (Jurvetson and Draper 1997).[5] However, the marketing literature has focused on "viral marketing" as a *strategy*. Kirby and Marsden (2012) distinguish between the marketing *strategies* of buzz, word-of-mouth (WOM), and virality, but as of yet, no one has offered a rigorous conceptualization of virality itself, as a process, let alone distinguished it from other information flow processes such as memes and cascades. The focus on the strategy of viral marketing has allowed marketing and network theory researchers to study the creation of viral campaigns (Phelps et al. 2004), modeling and predicting their spread and contagion (Aral and Walker 2011, 2012; Bampo et al. 2008; De Bruyn and Lilien 2008; Leskovec et al. 2007a; Van der Lans et al. 2010), measuring return on investment (Ferguson 2008), and engaging and managing consumers in spreading marketing messages (Krishnamurthy 2001; Palka et al. 2009). This rich body of literature continues to grow, but scholars from other fields, practitioners, and the general public are likely to pose other questions and have different kinds of applications for the concept of virality.

Having a clear definition of virality will help researchers to be clear about the type of information flows they are studying. It also may give politicians and executives an understanding of the life cycle of virality so they can plan ahead during media storms. It can help artists and activists reach the audiences they hope to connect with. Identifying viral events might also help librarians and information professionals to determine what content they should curate and archive for future purposes. The interest in understanding the way virality operates in society is growing, and researchers are actively studying it. For example, in the field of political science, Wallsten (2010, 2011) was interested in the role of blogs in driving viral political videos during the 2008 U.S. Presidential election; Ancu (2010), a communication scholar, investigated the credibility that viewers assigned to online viral messages; and in the field of information science, Nahon et al. (2011) use time series data and econometric modeling to map the life cycle of virality within the blogosphere at the time of elections. In the field of knowledge management, Hemsley and Mason (2012) used virality as a conceptual tool to show that many traditional knowledge management models were out of date, given today's media environment. However, the ability of researchers to compare findings about virality from one study to another is limited because no shared definition or measuring practices exist.

In the remainder of the chapter we draw on network and diffusion theory, as well as examples from empirical studies in other fields, to explain each one of the four components of our definition of virality: (i) the human and social aspects of sharing information from one to another; (ii) the speed of viral spread; (iii) the reach in terms of the number of people exposed to the content; and (iv) the reach in terms of the distance the information travels by bridging multiple networks. We also identify some of the limitations of our, or any, definition of virality and try to clarify the distinctions between virality and other types of information flow events.

The viral process as a social information flow

To understand virality as a social information flow process, let's start by supposing that a single person posts a link to a video on her Facebook page and trace the spread. Each person exposed to the link makes two key decisions. First, they decide whether to watch the video or not. This decision is influenced by factors related to context, content, form, social forces, and the identity and stance of the people involved (Barzilai-Nahon 2008; Shifman 2012). For example, the identity of the poster, and whether or not the poster included a comment that framed the message in a way that the receiver found favorable, would affect whether or not the receiver decided to watch the video (Scheufele and Tewksbury 2007). The second decision that each exposed person would make is whether or not to share the message with other people. The effort of doing this with Facebook and Twitter is trivial: users simply click the Share (Facebook) or Retweet (Twitter) button, effectively broadcasting the message (or link) to their network. So the decision about sharing or not sharing is not about how hard it is to spread the information. Rather, it has to do with social factors. It has to do with the same kinds of social factors that influence how we share information when we meet with people. For example, because at some level we are all concerned about how others perceive us, what Goffman (1990) calls our *presentation of self*, we may avoid sharing something if we think that our image will be damaged when others see it. Likewise, we may decide not to share something because we don't want others to know about it; we can act as gatekeepers for our own networks. There are many reasons. We will explore these reasons for sharing more in chapters 3 and 4, but the point is that the same factors that are at play when we share or don't share information in daily social situations are likely the same ones at play online.

What is different online, with our highly linked social infrastructure, is that once this first round of followers sees the video, some will again repost the link to it, which can result in many people simultaneously broadcasting it into their networks in a kind of many-to-many communication. Walther et al. refer to this as mass-personal communication (2010: 21) and Castells calls this mass self-communication (2009: 55). Instead of a televised broadcast from a single channel (one-to-many communication), or a WOM, interpersonal communication process (one-to-one), virality leverages situations where many people are sharing with many other people all at the same time. At each step out from the origin, another round of individuals, all of whom have their own broadcast capability, is exposed to the message.[6] One of the most fundamental reasons why we see virality as having a societal impact is that it is dependent on the social interactions of many people, a topic we will discuss in depth in chapter 6.

We mentioned in chapter 1 that the growth in the number of people who have seen the video is characterized by a slow-fast-slow signature (the growth pattern). This is illustrated in figure 2.1 with an S-shaped curve, or what's known as a *sigmoid curve*. At first, the growth within the network is relatively slow, but then it speeds up. As more and more people see the video and rebroadcast it in their own networks, the rate at which additional people are exposed also grows. This is captured in the first half of figure 2.1.

The S-shaped curve is similar to models of diffusion of technological innovation (Rogers 2003), as well as many epidemic models (Arneson 2006; Boynton 2009; Dicker et al. 2006; Mahajan and Peterson 1985; Pastor-Satorras and Vespignani 2001; Valente 1996). Rogers claims that a critical mass needs to occur for the diffusion of innovations to become self-sustaining (see figure 2.1). Gladwell refers to it as the "tipping point" (2002). This is the point where the number of people, coupled with the inertia of diffusion, helps to

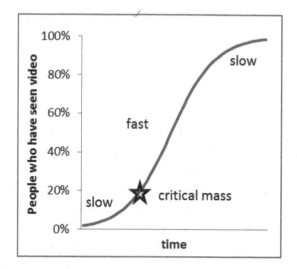

Figure 2.1: Sigmoid curve

propel the innovation deeply into a network. At some point in the diffusion process, the number of people who are likely to be exposed to the video for the first time begins to slow: there are fewer and fewer people who have not yet seen the video, and so the growth slows.

Let's apply this to the "United Breaks Guitars" video, one of our example cases in chapter 1. In figure 2.2 we plot the total views as reported by blogs and can see, even using this rough collection method, that even though bloggers post at different times of the day and are in different regions, the trend in growth follows a sigmoid curve. The more common way to represent a viral signature is to plot the view count for each day (Broxton et al. 2010; Nahon et al. 2011). From figure 2.3 we can see that the United Breaks Guitars video

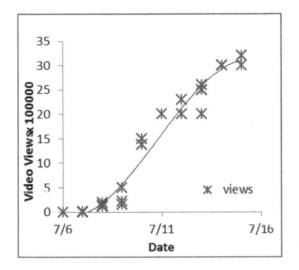

Figure 2.2: Blog reported cumulative views

exemplifies the life cycle of viral videos where the daily view count peaks in just a few days. Is a few days the typical time for a viral event to reach a peak? How fast does the information have to spread to be considered viral? Unfortunately, no specific number gives us a satisfying answer, which leads us to our discussion of viral speed.

Viral speed

Kwak et al. (2010) looked at 106 million tweets and found that half of all retweeting happens within the first hour of the origin tweet, and 75 percent within the first day. Looking at trending articles on Digg, a social news-sharing site, Wu and Huberman (2007) found that the

23

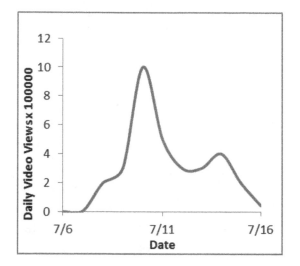

Figure 2.3: Daily views from blog reports

half-life for recommended stories was also about one hour, but Bakshy et al. (2012) found that the median time for resharing on Facebook was six hours, considerably longer, but still less than one day. These findings suggest that the majority of resharing happens within a day, but also that the rate of diffusion depends on the platform.

Additionally, Crane and Sornette (2008) demonstrate that the rate at which YouTube videos receive views effectively depends on how "social" the process was that drove viewers to the video (i.e., shared from person to person).[7] Importantly, they found that the number of views for *socially driven* videos ramped up to a peak and gradually decayed, whereas for less socially driven videos (e.g., a James Bond promotional movie trailer), views quickly spiked with little or no ramp-up time, and

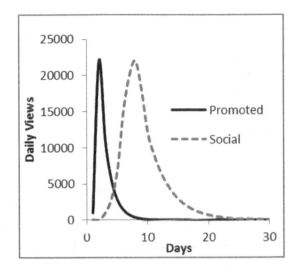

Figure 2.4: Social vs. promoted growth and decay

declined more sharply.[8] In other words, promoted messages tend to gain and lose the public's attention more quickly than socially driven messages, perhaps because social messages are more socially authentic. Figure 2.4 illustrates this by showing two hypothetical cases, one a social spread and the other a promoted spread. In chapters 3 and 4, when we discuss how virality occurs, we will show how the top-down promotional and bottom-up social processes work together to create different signatures. However, as we alluded to in the case of the Susan Boyle video, viral events are rarely either strictly promoted or strictly social.

There is a *sharp acceleration in the number of people who are exposed to the message* because there is a period of time early on in the social sharing process where the audience grows very rapidly due to a growth in many-to-many sharing. Here is how it works. Let's suppose that you are in Korea and playing a new smartphone game called *Anipang the Puzzle*. Through a popular instant message system, *Kakao Talk*, you let your friends know about the game. Let's also assume that five of your friends start playing and share the game with their friends in the first round. On round two, five people from each of your friend's network also start playing and again they spread it to their friends. If this continues for just five rounds, there would be 3,125 players. At each round the number of people who can share the content grows, so the audience grows quite fast indeed.[9] The dashed line in figure 2.4 would result from just this kind of sharing. These signature patterns are commonly found by researchers studying virality (Boynton 2009; Broxton et al. 2010; Nahon et al. 2011). But how can researchers know if the acceleration is fast enough to be considered a viral event? It turns out that if the decline in views, or *rate of decay*, is shaped like a *power-law distribution*,[10] you have a good candidate for a viral event[11] (see figure 2.5).

At the beginning of this chapter we asked: would the video "Librarians Do Gaga" be considered viral? Let's take a look. The video "Librarians Do Gaga" was produced by a graduate student at the University of Washington's Information School as part of a school film festival. The video is about a group of students and faculty making their library-style rendition of Lady Gaga's "Poker Face" and celebrating the importance of libraries. In figure 2.6 we see that the video's signature is similar to other viral events in that it starts slow then quickly gains views, then more gradually gains views.

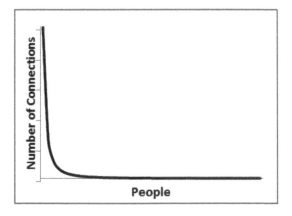

Figure 2.5: Example of a power-law distribution

Note that the tapering off of views is more similar to social sharing than promotion.[12] Even though this video didn't reach millions of people, like "United Breaks Guitars" or Susan Boyle's audition, we consider it viral because of the speed and way it spread, through social sharing processes. In fact, we can vouch for it being social because both of us received a link to the video, one through email and the other via Twitter, and forwarded it into our own networks after watching it. In the next section we will touch upon the question of how much reach information needs in order to be considered viral.

Before leaving the topic of speed, we also note that at the beginning of the chapter we asked if a math tutor video from the Kahn Academy that gained views at a fairly steady rate over two years would be considered viral. The answer is no because a steady rate of view growth would not exhibit a peak, followed by a decay

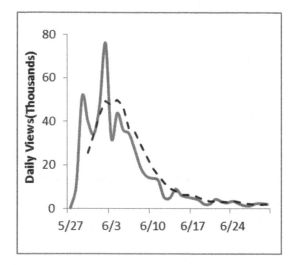

Figure 2.6: "Librarians Do Gaga"

phase that could be fitted to a power-law distribution. This video is an example of a *popular*, but not viral, video. Information items can be both viral and popular but would need to exhibit the typical peak and power-law decay phase discussed before to be considered viral.

So, does size matter? Virality is a process of diffusion and so the *way* it spreads, socially, during many-to-many communication, is more important than how many people actually end up seeing it. Virality is scalable. It can reach millions or it can reach hundreds. The "Librarians Do Gaga" video, delightful as it may be to the hundreds of thousands of librarians, friends of librarians, and educators, does not pull the same sort of universal emotional strings that "United Breaks Guitars" or Susan Boyle's triumph does. Surprising as it may be, not everyone can relate to librarians singing a Lady Gaga song between the stacks of the university library. However, since librarian's and their close information science friends feel strongly about the social value of libraries, they may actually be more likely to spread the video because they share a common niche *interest* that, to us, is worth celebrating. In other words, "Librarians Do Gaga" was a viral event in the community of information professionals.

Topical interest as a factor in the spread of virality is something we will return to very shortly. In fact, it is part of the final aspect of the viral process, which we cover in this chapter. The question at hand: how does virality achieve its deep reach into networks?

Viral reach (by numbers)

Reach refers to two distinct elements: (i) *reach by numbers*, the reach in terms of the number of people exposed to a content; (ii) *reach by networks*, the reach in terms of the distance the information travels by bridging multiple networks. Using the word "reach" in the context of social networks can be confusing because different people and companies use it to refer to different things. For example, some authors (Boynton 2009; Kwak et al. 2010) represent reach as the total number of people linked to all the people who forwarded a message. Such a method is simplistic and overstates the *actual reach* for five reasons:

1. *Life beyond the online*: Most users are not logged on constantly, limiting the number of friends or followers who may be exposed to any given message.

2. *Overlapping friends*: To understand overlap, we want to briefly introduce the concept of transitivity in social networks (Granovetter 1973): if A and B are strongly connected, and B and C are strongly connected, then A and C will likely develop a connection. The implication is that any two friends are likely to have some degree of overlap in their social networks because they often know some or many of the same people. So if A shares a news story and B shares the same story, C will likely see the story twice. On Facebook, where all ties are reciprocated, overlap will likely be higher than on Twitter, where research has shown that only 22 percent of ties are reciprocal.

3. *Selectivity*: Recent work has shown that people tend to retweet selectively (Kwak et al. 2010). This suggests that people pay attention to some people in their networks more than others, and so some messages will be ignored simply because of who sent it.

4. *Algorithmic gatekeeping*: Many social networks use algorithms to promote certain content over others. For example, Facebook will sort the top stories in your feed for you based on algorithms designed to highlight stories it thinks you will be interested in as well as those that are being *promoted* because someone has paid Facebook to promote them.[13]

5. *Repetitions*: Even when a platform does report the number of times content was viewed, like YouTube, this can still be misleading. One of us, for example, admits to having watched the librarian video at least 30 times.

By reach, with respect to the numbers, we mean both the people who saw the video or image, read the tweet or post, or otherwise consumed digital content, but did not share it, as well as all the people who did reshare it. This is an important distinction because as researchers we can rarely measure the exact reach.

Viral reach (by networks)

In most cases, reach-by-numbers is only part of the story. Viral events also reach deep into networks. Jurvetson, one of the early writers on viral marketing, wrote of the spread of HotMail that they "would notice the first user from an overseas university town, and then the number of subscribers from that region would rapidly proliferate" (2000: 110). What he is describing is how HotMail was first picked up by one user in a *cluster*, a sub-network where the people are tightly connected, who then influenced others in the cluster to adopt HotMail. In this way, the cluster becomes *saturated*, meaning the people who could potentially adopt, have done so. People in this cluster then influence people in other clusters to adopt, who then influence the people in their own clusters to adopt, saturating those clusters . . . and on and on in a pattern of local saturation, hop, saturation, hop.

It generally follows this pattern because people within clusters tend to have stronger ties and be more similar to each other than those in other clusters. Because people in clusters tend to be like-minded and have a relatively high degree of network overlap, messages spread quickly and easily within clusters. The spaces between the clusters, where links are sparse, are called network holes and are typically bridged by *weak ties* (Burt 2004). It is these weak ties that allow messages to move from one cluster of people to new audiences, where it might be further propagated.

Who are the weak ties? This is an important question because research shows that individuals are more likely to receive novel ideas from weak ties than from strong ties (Bakshy et al. 2012; Barabasi 2003; Burt 2004; Centola and Macy 2005; Granovetter 1973). For the purpose of the discussion here, a weak tie is, for example, an old friend from high school or a past job. Maybe they are someone who is a friend of a friend that you run into frequently enough so you know their name and can engage in conversation with them. Alternately, strong ties are our family, close friends, perhaps people we work with and see every day.

Sites such as Facebook allow people to maintain a larger set of weak ties than non-Facebook users (Ellison et al. 2010). If you use Facebook, you may have gone through a phase early on where you connected to people you went to school with or worked with at a previous job, but otherwise have not seen for years. In some cases, you didn't even know them and connected to them only because of shared interests. It is from these weak ties that new content originates. If we like content we get from weak ties and reshare it, other people in our own cluster, who are similar to us, may also like it. Our resharing can saturate our local cluster of close ties. Also, people who follow us, that consider us a weak tie, may find the content compelling and interesting and reshare it into their own cluster of close friends where it can again saturate, spread, saturate.

This begs the question: at what point do we say information has flowed through enough clusters that it is viral? The answer is not a specific number but, as we noted earlier, it is the point when a critical mass or tipping point is reached (see figure 2.1). The rate of sharing (speed), number of clusters (reach), and the degree that people are connected to different clusters all work together to drive something to and beyond the tipping point. Once the tipping point is passed, the content has enough momentum that it is propelled far beyond a local set of clusters into the wider network.[14]

Saturation of a network does not mean that everyone in the network engages with the message. Of those who read a post or watch a video, not everyone will forward it (Huberman and Adamic 2004), effectively filtering content for their own networks in a process that Shirky (2009) refers to as *filter forwarding* and Barzilai-Nahon as *network gatekeeping* (2008, 2009). Followers engage with posts for any number of reasons, at some of which we have already hinted. One reason to engage with a post is the concept of "communicator utility," which suggests that sometimes people engage with content, so that they have something to talk about with someone they want to talk to (Walther et al. 2010). As an example, if Karine posts a link to a video, Jeff may watch the video because he is interested in talking with Karine, not because he is interested in the content. So the filter forward decision is also influenced by our knowledge of the sender and our relationship with them.

But *interest* can work in another way. We are

generally unaware of all of the *interests* of our weak ties, so when they post something, it may unexpectedly be of interest to us. In such a case, the information has the potential to hop from their cluster to ours and so on, following links between people who are interested in the content or the people posting the content. Allsop et al. note that a viral spread "happens in the context of a specific situation and occasion" (2007: 402), which implies that these events are topically and temporally bound. In fact, if we could trace the forwarding of content, from user-to-user and cluster-to-cluster, it would create a short-lived interest network. Thus, *a viral information event creates a temporally bound, self-organized, interest network in which membership is based on an interest in the information content or in belonging to the interest network of others.* So the reach that we are discussing refers to everyone with an interest in the content who can be connected to the interest network, not the potential reach. It is all of the people who engaged with the content, whether they forwarded it or not.

The concept of an interest network is an important one that we will revisit in later chapters. However, the idea that people self-select content based on interest, coupled with the reach of virality, means that people may be exposed to ideas and information that they otherwise wouldn't be. Hemsley and Mason (2012) note that interest networks, that are repeatedly invoked, may transform latent ties into durable social networks focused around a specific topic. As bonding relationships among members of the network continue to develop (Nahapiet and Ghoshal 1998), productive communities of practice (Wenger 1998) may form. The implication is that viral events can help bring people together for common interests, purposes, or actions. In chapter 4 we will elaborate on this more, but the key point is that virality is ephemeral and contextual: a video about a politician may go viral during their campaign, but could be a dud ten years later if they don't stay in the public eye.

What virality isn't

Before we move on to discuss how virality works, we will briefly introduce three other important concepts that we want to differentiate from virality. These are word-of-mouth (WOM), memes, and information cascades. Each of these terms has their own histories and has been developed in different bodies of literature. Depending on the body of literature one reads, they are often used interchangeably or ambiguously. For example, a great deal of marketing literature has tended to see virality as a specific kind of WOM instead of as a distinct process in its own right (De Bruyn and Lilien 2008; Dobele et al. 2005; Golan and Zaidner 2008; Helm 2000; Leskovec et al. 2007a; Palka et al. 2009; Van der Lans et al. 2010).

Also, in the case of virality and memes, Jenkins (2009) argues that currently the use of these metaphors wrongfully implies that people are passive and without individual or social agency. In other words, the biological roots of the word viral suggest that people can be unaware of, or have little choice about, being infected and transmitting media messages. His solution

35

is to escape the terms *meme* and *viral information*, and instead to adopt the concept of "spreadable media" for both constructs. However, as we will explain below, these two concepts are different. Distinguishing between them allows researchers to answer questions about the effects of viral vs. non-viral memes, or the different factors that drive viral vs. non-viral memes. Finally, some researchers use the phrase *information cascades* to describe the way information spreads in networks (Leskovec et al. 2007b). On the surface, this might seem appropriate, but has several problems, the most obvious being that a cascade need not achieve any sort of critical mass.

In the next few paragraphs we will first give a brief overview of what word-of-mouth (WOM), memes, and information cascades are, and then summarize how they are similar and distinct from viral events.

Word-of-mouth

We mentioned earlier in the chapter that marketers use the term virality to define a strategy for getting consumers to tell others about a product, as it has long been recognized that word-of-mouth (WOM) marketing is more influential than advertising over the airwaves. So for them, virality induces WOM. But the fundamental idea of WOM is that people speak to each other, often about a product, but without a commercial motive.[15] Word of mouth is not a network process in itself, but does assume personal interaction between people, while virality must employ the many-to-many, mass-personal communication we described above. For us, the viral process may indeed induce WOM, but WOM is not necessarily the process by which viral diffusion occurs. Also, other key aspects of virality are its speed and reach-by-numbers and reach-by-networks, which are not required elements of WOM.

Memes

Memes are defined as units of culture that spread from person to person by copying or imitation (Shifman 2012, 2013). Given the way we have defined a viral event, there is no reason to think that a meme couldn't go viral in the form of a *viral topic*, as many posts and shares about the same *topic* that together interact and feed off of each other in a digitally mediated conversation. In terms of their speed and reach, viral topics are similar to viral events. The difference is simply that we would refer to a single item (video, tweet, game, news story, etc.) as a viral event, and an emerging or trending topic with viral features as a viral topic. These distinctions are, however, new and as researchers we might like to know if memes are generally the result of viral events. For example, in chapter 1, we discussed the viral photographs of Lt. Pike casually pepper-spraying peaceful student protestors. Very quickly after these photos started to circulate, people began creating images that remixed the key aspects into new situations – for example, Lt. Pike inserted into the *Last Supper* painting, Pike spraying *My Little Pony* characters, tiny Lego models reconstructing the scene, Pike spraying the U.S. founding fathers, and many others.[16] Another difference is in how scholars study a particular bit of content. When we look at viral events, we are mainly interested in the information event: how it spreads, the effects of the spread, and possibly why one spreads but not another. Researchers into memetics are typically more focused on understanding the transition from the original content to its derivatives, comparing memes, or looking for common elements.

Information cascades

Cascades are a concept used to explain why people imitate other people's behaviors. Information cascades have been an important area of research in the field of economics and management since Bikhchandani et al. (1992) published an influential paper, claiming that fads, fashion, and other cultural change processes could be explained by information cascades. For them, people can *follow the herd* or *jump on the bandwagon* when people mimic other people's behavior. Have you ever seen a line of people waiting by a door that you knew was unlocked? The first person assumed the door was locked, so they waited outside. The second person saw the first person and assumed that they had already checked to see if the door was open. Each additional person would make the same assumption, that someone in the growing line would have already checked the door, and so they too would get in line. In this example, people abandon their own impulse to check the door, and follow the herd. Unlike virality, this does not have to happen quickly or reach many people. When researchers use the concept of information cascades to explain information flows, they are assuming that people watch and share content solely because other people have watched and shared the content. However, that is only part of the story. Research has suggested

Table 2.1: Distinguishing related concepts from virality

	Social sharing	Sharp acceleration	Reach-by-numbers	Reach-by-networks
Virality	Yes	Yes	Yes	Yes
WOM	Yes	Not required	Not required	Not required
Meme	Yes	Not required	Not required	Not required
Information cascade	No	Not required	Not required	Not required

that people are selective when it comes to consuming information (Huberman and Adamic 2004; Kwak et al. 2010), and that people share messages for a variety of reasons (boyd et al. 2010), some of which we will discuss in chapter 4. So, like memes, a viral event can have some element of cascading behavior, but information cascades do not necessarily display the speed and reach we find in viral events.

Table 2.1 summarizes the similarities and differences among the concepts of virality, WOM, memes, and information cascades. The columns in table 2.1 represent the core elements needed for something to be considered a viral event.

Moving on

The key conceptual elements of virality, as we have discussed in this chapter, are:

1. *the human and social aspects of information sharing from one to another*;
2. *the speed of spread*;

3. *the reach in terms of the number of people exposed to the content*; and
4. *the reach in terms of the distance the information travels by bridging multiple networks.*

The characterization of viral events as described in this chapter is an idealized version of viral events. The majority of viral events are a result of both top-down and bottom-up processes. Many viral items are derivatives, responses, or copies of content generated by the mass-media producers that the public has found interesting or entertaining enough to share (Asur et al. 2011; Burgess and Green 2009; Crane and Sornette 2008; Kwak et al. 2010). In other words, social media and mass media interact. A conversation may start in Twitter, spread across social media platforms, be reported on by the mainstream media, which may result in further attention throughout social media as people discuss and collectively make sense of the media's response. But for content to be considered viral, it needs to spread in networks as a result of social sharing processes even if it has also been promoted. We will discuss this further in chapters 3 and 4. In this chapter we have also given some hints at how the viral process works. It is time to go deeper and explore some well-known examples in an attempt to understand the mechanics of what makes something *go viral*.

3

What Makes Something Viral I: The control of networks through gatekeeping

Now that we have a sense for recognizing content that has gone viral, we will spend the next three chapters focusing on the factors that *make* something go viral. The first key question for this part of the book is why does one video get millions of views, while millions of videos only get a few views?

As we have indicated before, virality is a complex process. One way to understand it is to break it into parts, understand the parts, and then tie it all together. We have already started to do this by alluding to *top-down* and *bottom-up* forces as the drivers of virality, but as with any conceptual breakdown, this is an imperfect division. For example, we discussed *promotion* of content as a top-down force in both chapters 1 and 2, but we can easily imagine grass-roots, or bottom-up, promotion efforts. So, while any conceptual breakdown of a complex process is far from perfect, we think that using the top-down/bottom-up dichotomy is helpful in terms of presenting the ideas of this chapter as well as in chapter 4. In chapter 5 we will show that the top and bottom blur together, shaping with the structures of networks the nature of virality. Chapter 5 will also be where we discuss whether or not the process of virality can be designed and controlled.

Our concept of top-down forces refers to the promotional efforts that we have already discussed, as well as *network gatekeeping*, which we will explore in this chapter. These top-down forces arise out of the ability of powerful foci (actors or institutions) to drive viral information flows in networks. The bottom-up perspective, which is the focus of chapter 4, is made up of patterns of human attention and sharing, as well as how we influence each other within our immediate networks, and refers to the impact of people's actions on whether or not something goes viral as they create, consume, and share content.

Our use of a "top-down" perspective for information flows is not new. Katz and Lazarsfeld (1955) looked at opinion leaders in their two-step flow of communication and Tushman and Katz (1980) highlighted the role of boundary spanners, "key individual(s) who are both strongly connected to internal colleagues and strongly linked to external domains" in information flows. Metoyer-Duran's work discusses cultural gatekeepers, who are individuals that "actively participate in the information-retrieval and dissemination process in their communities" (1993: 119) and how they are *designated* by their communities (Metoyer-Duran 1991). Also, Barzilai-Nahon (2008, 2009) has developed the concept of network gatekeepers, which we draw on for this chapter. There are nuanced differences in the ways researchers have used the various terms, but one common element is that certain actors can exercise greater control over the flow of information than others, and as such, they have a disproportionate amount of influence. Also scientists have shown that the structure of networks plays an important role in how, and the degree to which, information spreads. For example, Barabasi (2003) uses mathematical models to show that many social networks are scale free, which means that the number of connections of people follows a power-law distribution (a few nodes have many connections while most have relatively few), which supports the idea that the attention of the masses is concentrated on a few influential actors, who can be referred to as hubs or gatekeepers. These concepts about structure will be covered in chapter 5.

Network gatekeepers have a tremendous impact on information flows: by choosing which information can or cannot pass, by connecting networks or clusters to one another, or in general by regulating the movement of information. Who are these network gatekeepers and how do they impact virality? Network gatekeepers (people, collectives, or institutions) are those with the discretion to control information as it flows in and among networks. They can choose which information they let flow and which information they withhold, and more generally they can choose the extent to which gatekeeping is exercised. However, their power is not absolute and their impact depends to a large extent on the gated, those subjected to their gatekeeping (Barzilai-Nahon 2008, 2009; Nahon 2011). To make it more complicated, their role is dynamic and changeable. Gatekeepers can gain or lose power; they can become

gated and the gated can become gatekeepers. To understand what this all means, let's suppose that Jeff (*the
gated*) has a Facebook account and posts a message on
his timeline. Facebook exercises gatekeeping power in
the form of controlling the flow of information by chan-
neling, ranking, and promoting particular content over
other content in the news feed of Jeff's friends. In fact,
Facebook can decide to censor and delete a post, if it
runs against their terms of service. Facebook can use its
gatekeeping power efficiently and have a major impact
on people, because Jeff and millions of other people
have decided to use it as a social network platform. If
Facebook lost its ability to hold our *attention*, a scarce
resource in our world today, it would also lose its power
to exercise gatekeeping. To help us better understand
the role of gatekeeping in viral events, let us look at
virality in the context of the spread of the news about
the death of Osama bin Laden (introduced in chapter
1). Exploring this case again will give us an opportunity
to highlight the different types of gatekeepers and how
their actions can make or break viral events.

In chapter 1 we gave a general overview of the case
of Keith Urbahn's viral tweet that effectively announced
the death of Osama bin Laden. What we want to do
now is focus on the role of specific individuals in spreading the information. The milestones relevant to our
analysis are presented in table 3.1.

Once Dan Pfeiffer, the person behind the official
Twitter account of the White House, announced that
President Obama would address the nation, rumors
began circulating on Twitter and other platforms. Some,
which included a fair amount of banter, speculated that

Table 3.1: Information flow milestones in the Keith Urbahn case (May 1, 2011)

Time (EDT)	Event
21:46	Dan Pfeiffer, from the White House official twitter account, tweets: "POTUS to address the nation tonight at 10:30 PM Eastern Time"
21:46	First speculation about the topic of the President's address
22:24	Keith Urbahn tweets: "So I'm told by a reputable person they have killed Osama Bin Laden. Hot damn."
22:25	Brian Stelter retweets: "Chief of staff for former defense sec. Rumsfeld, @keithurbahn, tweets: 'I'm told by a reputable person they have killed Osama Bin Laden.'"
22:40	Media confirms the news (single line running across the bottom of TV screen)
22:45	Three channels (ABC, CBS, and NBC) broadcast the news
23:35	US President Obama addresses the nation in a press conference

it was about Osama bin Laden, while others suspected it was about Muammar Gaddafi, former ruler of Libya (Lotan and Gaffney 2011). None of these rumors caught on. In his role as the director of communications for the White House, Dan Pfeiffer is a perfect example of a traditional information gatekeeper, one that selects what information other people see. It seems highly likely that he knew what the announcement was about, but withheld that information from the public. He had good reason. As President, Commander-in-Chief, as well as the man responsible for ordering the raid on bin Laden, it was President Obama's responsibility to make the announcement, which illustrates the power of traditional gatekeepers as having control of when or if information is released. We often tend to think of information selection as what traditional gatekeepers do. Since they are recognized as a central source of information, as was Dan Pfeiffer, they can suppress information, but at the same time have the power to open the gates and let particular information go through. But it doesn't end there. If Dan Pfeiffer worked in our local grocery store as a cashier, he likely wouldn't be able to muster the same audience as he can in his role as director of communications for the White House. In other words, it is his position that brings him an audience (Metoyer-Duran 1993). Therefore, the identity of an information source plays a crucial role in the viral process.

At 22:24:05 p.m. (EDT), 38 minutes after Dan Pfeiffer's tweet, Keith Urbahn posted his now-famous tweet, shown in figure 3.1. His position as Donald Rumsfeld's chief of staff gave him and his tweet enough *credibility* to overcome the rumors and ignite the viral process on Twitter. By credibility we mean that he was a believable and trusted source of information. Research has shown that subjects are more likely to adopt a source's position if that source is seen as credible (Hovland and Weiss 1951). We can see the claim of credibility in Brian Stelter's modified tweet when he invokes Donald Rumsfeld's name at the start of his post, implying that Rumsfeld himself is behind that tweet (figure 3.2). Also, note that Brian Stelter is a media reporter for *The New York Times*, which lends additional credibility to the message.

For something to be considered viral we need to examine the social information exchange among people.

Keith Urbahn
@keithurbahn

So I'm told by a reputable person they have killed Osama Bin Laden. Hot damn.

← Reply ⇄ Retweet ★ Favorite

Figure 3.1: Keith Urbahn's tweet

Brian Stelter ☑
@brianstelter

Chief of staff for former defense sec. Rumsfeld, @kcithurbahn, tweets: "I'm told by a reputable person they have killed Osama Bin Laden."

← Reply ⇄ Retweet ★ Favorite

Figure 3.2: Brian Stelter's tweet

In figure 3.3 we can see the signature of the viral event in terms of the speed and the social sharing.[1] The graph represents the flow of information as captured by retweets, and as such notes how many people have spread the content but grossly underestimates how many people actually saw the tweet.[2] In any event, there is almost no ramp-up time – the event quickly gains traction, peaks, and then decays. Rumors had been circulating for more than half an hour, some of which had been about capturing or killing Osama bin Laden. The credibility of the message was all it needed for it to take off. This is part of what we mean when we say that virality depends on context. If Keith Urbahn had sent the same message half an hour before the announcement that the President was going to address the nation, it may not have taken off the way it did.

Figure 3.4 is a network plot of the retweets in the

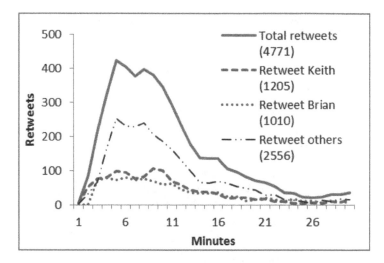

Figure 3.3: Total retweets and direct retweets

event. It captures the signature of the viral event in terms of the reach and social sharing. If you take a look you will see that there are many direct retweets from both Keith Urbahn and Brian Stelter, and that there are waves of social sharing that bring the viral message to distant parts of the network.

While traditional gatekeeping focuses mainly on selection (e.g., editors of journals who decide what to publish in the newspapers), network gatekeepers have many additional information control mechanisms. The power of network gatekeepers does not necessarily reside in the ability to stop information from getting to people or by filtering it. On the contrary, it is hidden in their ability to link networks together, allowing information to travel far and fast and to connect people to information and ideas. This is the key to social transformation in networked societies.

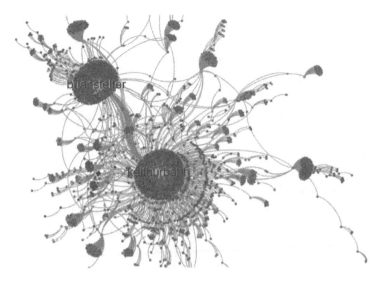

Figure 3.4: Social network visualization of Keith Urbahn tweet

Keith Urbahn and Brian Stelter represent two different types of gatekeepers. As Donald Rumsfeld's Chief of Staff, Keith Urbahn held a position similar to Dan Pfeiffer: a traditional gatekeeper who could withhold or let flow information. Also, part of his audience was likely made up of people who saw him as a reliable source of information, a gatekeeper, or sometimes we might refer to people in this kind of position as *a person in the know*. But he had 1,016 followers[3] at the time of his tweet, whereas Brian Stelter had more than 50,000 followers. As a journalist who can decide to report or not report some information, Brian Stelter had the same traditional gatekeeping power, but he is also a good example of what we refer to as a network gatekeeper. The power of a network gatekeeper also lies in their ability to facilitate information flows and to bridge many networks. Brian Stelter's large network enabled the information to travel to other networks that are far beyond the reach of Keith Urbahn.

Who's tweet was more influential? It depends. The impression from looking at figures 3.3 and 3.4 is that Keith Urbahn's tweet was more influential. In figure 3.3 we can see that even though he had far fewer followers than Brian Stelter, more people retweeted his original tweet. Also, from figure 3.4, we can see that Keith Urbahn's tweet sparked more and deeper waves of retweets. However, these plots only represent a small part of the story and we need to look at the larger context to be able to answer this question. Like all viral events, this one occurred within a larger media context, one where Brian Stelter was a well-known journalist.

Attracting the attention of others is the name of the game for network gatekeeping. Content will spread if people know it is available to be spread, and gatekeepers bring content to the attention of those who follow them. They become hubs of power in networks. The Brian Stelters of the world can exercise gatekeeping effectively because we pay attention to them. If his ability to provide insightful news or being perceived as trustworthy were to diminish, people would start following someone else and his power would decline. Since we have so many different content options today, network gatekeepers must constantly work to keep the attention of a fickle public. So networks are as dynamic as human relationships or human attention, and a network gatekeeper's role is never guaranteed.

The other important feature of network gatekeepers is that they can simultaneously be a gatekeeper and, in a different role, gated. Keith Urbahn is an example of this. If Dan Pfeiffer had not sent his tweet about the Presidential message, which created the rumor mill we mentioned, we doubt that Keith Urbahn's tweet would have spread the way it did without someone like Brian Stelter to retweet it. In other words, with his 1,016 followers it is likely he was not well connected enough to start an event that would reach and surpass a tipping point. However, even without the context of the rumors and expected Presidential announcement, a retweet of Keith's news about bin Laden from Brian likely would have reached enough clusters to propel it past a tipping point. In this way, Keith can be thought of as *gated*, but it also implies that *context is key in determining who is gated and when*.

Let's return to our example with another graph that will help us understand the media context within which our viral case took place. Figure 3.5, released by Twitter, shows the total number of tweets per second from 9:30 p.m. to 12:30 a.m., eastern standard time.[4] First, note that even though more than 4,500 people retweeted Keith Urbahn's tweet, the volume is hardly noticeable given the total volume of Twitter traffic. Second, traffic in the Twitter-sphere started its geometric increase right about 10:40 p.m., the time the mainstream media began to confirm the story online. At 10:40, *The New York Times*' national security team and its Washington bureau decided to run a one-line mention of bin Laden's death on the Internet.[5] At 10:44 p.m. *The New York Times* tweeted, "NYT NEWS ALERT: Osama bin Laden Is Dead, White House Says," and the volume of tweets exploded and continued to rise as ABC, NBC, and CBS all reported the story.

51

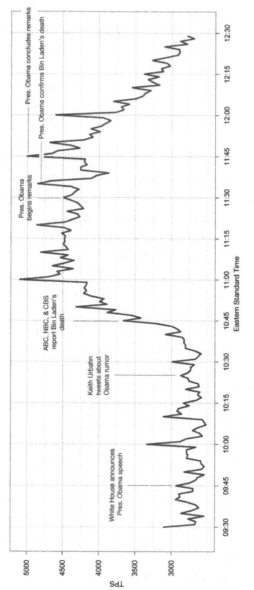

Figure 3.5: Tweets-per-second traffic (May 1, 2011)

52

Typically the media would have waited for the President to make the announcement, but the data suggests that the viral event may have nudged the traditional media into reporting, and thus confirming the story earlier than they would have (Hu et al. 2012). SocialFlow's analysis suggests that as many as 15 million tweets about bin Laden's death had been sent between the time of Dan Pfeiffer's tweet and when the President addressed the nation. Not shown on this graph is that it was the mainstream media's coverage that reached the majority of households; PEJ reports that the coverage of the raid accounted for 69 percent of the newshole, a journalism measure for how much space or time a story gets, during the week after the attack (May 2–8) (Holocomb 2011).

From our discussion and graphs, it is clear that Keith Urbhan's tweet went viral, and in the days following the event, many news reports and bloggers credited Keith Urbahn with breaking the story.[6] The vast majority of Americans learned about Osama bin Laden's death from a traditional news source, like CNN, ABC, CBS, or Fox News. These media channels have been in a gatekeeper role for decades, but their individual gatekeeping power has diminished as more channels have emerged. For example, Kirby and Marsden (2012) note that in 1965 the number of prime time spots an advertiser would need to reach 80 percent of the adult population in the U.S. was three, but in 2002 the number was 117. Thus, today's gatekeepers are gatekeepers partly because people pay attention to them.

There are two last points we want to make about this case before briefly summarizing our discussion of the role of gatekeepers in viral events: one, the case of Keith

Urbahn's viral tweet is also a case of a viral topic, where the topic itself becomes viral and is composed of many viral and non-viral events; second, the flow of information can sometimes start in social media before being reported in the mainstream press.

Recall that the viral event happened within the context of a bubbling rumor mill, so there were already discussions about what the President was going to report. In figure 3.5, we don't see evidence of the rumors significantly affecting the volume of tweets, but within a few minutes of Urbahn's tweet, the volume starts to rise. In figure 3.3, we can see the activity around Urbahn's tweet had diminished, but the tweets-per-second in figure 3.5 is still ramping up. Very quickly an enormous number of tweets emerged around the topic of the death of Osama bin Laden. Urbahn's tweet likely triggered the viral topic, which peaked around 11:00 p.m. and decayed over time.

Let's suppose that no one on Twitter or elsewhere in social media broke the story before the President's announcement on TV. If this had been the case, we believe that a viral topic would have emerged anyway as a result of the significance of the event, existing rumors, the structure of networks, and humans' propensity to share information. Urbahn's tweet may have sparked this viral topic, but the fact that the news coverage of the raid accounted for 69 percent of the newshole for the week after the attack indicates it would have been a very hot viral topic no matter who broke the news.

The case of Urbahn's tweet is also an example of a viral event on social media that preceded reporting on mainstream media. Many studies have noted that a majority of content that circulates on social media is copied or a derivative of mainstream media content (Asur et al. 2011; Burgess and Green 2009; Crane and Sornette 2008; Kwak et al. 2010). Also, Leskovec et al. (2009) followed quoted phrases and found that diffusion from news media to blogs was more common than from blogs to news media. But as our case exemplifies, the flow can go the other way. In other studies, Drezner and Farrell (2008) found that political journalists often read the top political blogs in an effort to discern important trending topics, and the work of our own Social Media Lab (SoMe Lab) at the University of Washington on the media and Twitter flows around the Occupy Wall Street movement suggests that certain types of events are more likely to start diffusing in social media and then get reported on in the mainstream media later (Nahon et al. 2013).

Network gatekeepers and these non-traditional information flows challenge traditional gatekeepers, like the media, by introducing competition and alternatives to choose other sources of information that flow on different paths. These alternatives limit any gatekeepers from having absolute control over the flow of information. Pew Research Center has shown that the credibility of newspapers, cable, and local news as well as network news has all been on the decline. Organizations like Fox and MSNBC have fallen from 67 and 73 percent positive marks in 2002 to 49 and 50 percent in 2012, respectively (Pew Research Center, 2012b). Additionally, Hu et al.'s (2012) work showed that audience certainty did not reach 80 percent until the mainstream media confirmed the report. Their work also showed that after Keith Urbahn's tweet, the sense of certainty in tweet texts rose to over 50 percent and generally increased until the TV media's confirmation of Osama bin Laden's death. In chapter 6 we will discuss how these challenges to traditional gatekeepers are one aspect of the way viral events can change our social landscape.

Why do so many people still tune into a TV station like ABC, when so many other sources of information exist? Why do people rely on gatekeepers? One answer has to do with the credibility that we've already mentioned. In general, people still turn to traditional media for confirmation. Hu et al. (2012) confirmed that it wasn't until the mainstream media reported on bin Laden's death that the percentage of tweets conveying certainty rose to and stayed above 80 percent. Another answer has to do with information overload, which we have mentioned briefly before. With the abundant number of information channels, people could quickly become overwhelmed without some sort of selection strategy.

There are a number of ways people deal with information overload. Two reasons relevant to our discussion of gatekeepers are, first, people tend to select information sources that provide content that they agree with (McPherson et al. 2001; Sunstein 2001). This is partly due to the idea that information that challenges our view of the world is more difficult to cognitively digest than information we already have a framework for. One result is that once people find a source that they are comfortable with, they will generally stick with it. The second reason people select gatekeepers to overcome information overload is related to the idea that with so much information out there, finding the *right* information is costly in terms of time and effort, so people engage in *satisficing*. Satisficing is the idea that once we have something *good enough*, based on whatever criteria we think is important, we stop searching. When people are faced with constraints, such as having time limits, they do not seek perfect solutions but solutions that are good enough; satisficing ones. Our attention is one of today's most scarce resources and we often, consciously or unconsciously, select gatekeepers of different types to help us filter information in an effort to prevent overload. Once we select a gatekeeper, we may habitually continue to select them because finding an alternative is time consuming. This implies that in some cases gatekeepers can benefit from a kind of momentum: once they have an audience, switching costs may inhibit members of their audience from seeking out alternates.

It is important to realize that the traditional media are not the only gatekeepers in our lives. Every activity we engage in while we are online – every link we follow, every page we download, every video we watch – has passed through some sort of gatekeepers. Browsers help us navigate our way around the web, search engines help us find relevant information, social network sites display the newsfeed of our friends, and blogs present content we are interested in. But every tool we use while on the Internet is a type of gatekeeper. The browser is made by an organization that makes choices about what kinds of content the browser will support. Search engines serve up content based on their own criteria of what is relevant. Sites like Facebook use algorithms to decide what content we will be interested in. Blogging tools support certain content and make presenting other content more difficult. By using these tools we implicitly accept the rules designed into the tools by the organizations that created them.

For now, we want to summarize our discussion of gatekeepers and their role in the case of Keith Urbahn's tweet before moving on to the next chapter, where we examine the bottom-up forces that also drive virality. We have noted that both Dan Pfeiffer and Keith Urbahn acted as traditional gatekeepers as they were in a position to withhold or let flow information. Dan Pfeiffer held that position as a result of his being the White House's *designated* gatekeeper, but for Keith Urbahn it was dependent on the context of the event, which highlights the dynamic nature of gatekeepers. Brian Stelter acted as a network gatekeeper by linking clusters together and helping Keith's tweet reach distant clusters in the network. We noted that the traditional media plays both roles – traditional and network gatekeeper – but enjoys that position in part by producing content that holds the attention of a public, and in part because switching costs can create a kind of momentum where audience members tune in out of habit. Despite this, the public can be fickle and has many other options, so the role of a gatekeeper is never guaranteed. Also, whereas 30 years ago traditional gatekeepers could just withhold content if they chose, viral events spread in social media and circumvent traditional gatekeeping channels. This reduces, but does not eliminate, some forms of gatekeeping power, so today's traditional gatekeepers must do what they can to hold our attention. Finally, though we haven't mentioned it yet, every person who retweeted Keith's tweet engaged in a form of gatekeeping when they received the news and made a decision to retweet or not to retweet the content.

No matter how much power gatekeepers have, virality is a social process that requires people to share content with each other. Gatekeepers can broadcast content, thereby linking networks, but unless some of the people who engage with the content find it remarkable enough to pass along to their friends, followers, and families, it isn't a viral event. In the next chapter, we explore some of the reasons why people share content and discuss the role of personal influence in spreading viral messages. Along the way we show how remarkable content can form interest networks, which will be an important concept that we use when discussing the ways viral events are transforming our society in chapter 6.

4

What Makes Something Viral II: What is everyone looking at?

In the last chapter we explored network gatekeeping as a top-down force that can drive virality by connecting networks and choosing content to present. But this is only part of the story. It is the gated, or the audience, that constitutes gatekeepers through their collective patterns (Nahon 2011). In this chapter, we take a look at the bottom-up perspective and focus on content and how viral events emerge out of the patterns of human attention and personal influence. Some researchers argue that gatekeepers are not the most important factor in driving virality. For example, Watts and Dodds used mathematical modeling techniques to show that gatekeepers are not necessarily required for viral events. They say that in most situations, viral events "do not succeed because of a few highly influential individuals influencing everyone else but rather on account of a critical mass of easily influenced individuals influencing other easy-to-influence people" (2007: 454). Allsop et al. (2007) support this view with survey data that suggests that true cross-topic *influentials* are rare. Instead, different people are influentials in different categories. The picture emerging is that while gatekeepers are needed to make people aware of content, social interactions between people are also a fundamental aspect of viral events. Like chapter 3, we are addressing the question, why does one video get millions of views, while millions of videos only get a few views? In this chapter, we are looking at the question from a different angle by focusing on patterns of sharing behavior that are emerging.

The content must be remarkable!

The fields of sociology and psychology have long studied and developed theories to explain why people behave the way they do. Instead of delving deeply into these theories, we intend to provide concrete examples of several factors that have arisen in recent research as themes in viral events. Our coverage in this chapter is not exhaustive, but we would like to focus on emotional aspects, information characteristics, and context as factors that impact sharing, and show how they intermingle to make remarkable content. Why do people forward anything to their friends? We know that people are selective about what information they forward (Huberman and Adamic 2004), and from whom (Kwak et al. 2010). Also they are consistently aware of, and consider, their audience when they do forward content (boyd 2008). This implies that for something to go viral, it must not only get our attention in the first place, but it must overcome our resistance to sharing it. It must, as Kirby and Marsden (2012) say, be remarkable. It must be worth remarking on with the people we are connected to.

We start our exploration by revisiting the example of the viral video of Susan Boyle singing "I Dreamed a Dream" from chapter 1. People who forwarded the link of the Susan Boyle video did so because, for them, it was worth remarking on. What made it remarkable will be different from one person to the next. Letty Cottin Pogrebin, a blogger with a column at the Huffington Post, gives us some insight why she shared the video with her friends: the video had an emotional impact on her:

> But I'd wager that most of our joyful tears were fueled by the moral implicit in Susan's fairy-tale performance: "You can't tell a book by its cover." For such extraordinary artistry to emerge from a woman that plain-spoken, unglamorous, and unyoung was an intoxicating reminder of the wisdom in that corny old cliché. The three judges and virtually all those who watched Susan Boyle in the theater (and probably on YouTube as well) were initially blinded by entrenched stereotypes of age, class, gender, and Western beauty standards, until her book was opened and everyone saw what was inside. (Pogrebin 2009)

Not just for her, but for those she shared it with. People wrote back to her saying they had wept upon seeing Ms. Boyle get three 'Yes's from the judges. Emotional impact, then, is at least one reason why people will find the content remarkable enough to forward. This is supported by research (Bakshy et al. 2011) that has shown that content that elicits positive emotions is more likely to spread than content that does not.

Emotional aspects are one set of factors that can make content remarkable. But information characteristics, like humor, surprise, novelty, resonance, and quality, can influence our decision to share as well. The Boyle video was also a skillfully produced video designed to invoke surprise. This is set up by Boyle's appearance as "plain-spoken, unglamorous, and unyoung." The story is also set up when Boyle says she hopes to become a "professional singer" and the cameras zoom in on the faces of the judges and audience members whose expressions seem to indicate they are about to see a train wreck. First-time viewers of the video have no reason to suspect that Susan Boyle is truly a talented singer, and so, just as the audience does, they wince with foreboding. Then comes the surprise, echoed on the faces of the judges and audience: Boyle's voice is clear and strong and we can't help but wonder how that voice comes out of that woman, whom we have already stereotyped, perhaps as a result of being signaled to do so by the studio audience and judges. The story is fulfilled when, after her impressive performance, the judges, one after another, vote in her favor. Surprise, or novelty, seems to be a feature of many viral events.

The quality of the content, another information characteristic, is certainly another aspect. If you watched the Boyle video, you may remember Piers Morgan and Amanda Holden, the first two judges, gush with surprise and enthusiasm after Boyle finished singing. Simon Cowell, a TV producer and the show's third judge, claimed that he knew she would be great. The audience laughs and the other judges roll their eyes, and so we write his comment off as braggadocio. Was it? Pop culture critic Mark Blankenship (2009) writes that the video's "narrative is just as manipulative as anything else on reality television." His remarks imply that the video was skillfully produced and designed to have exactly the emotional effect it did. TV producers like Simon Cowell are certainly adept at creating content that captures people's attention.

Another example of high-quality content that went viral is David Carroll's video, "United Breaks Guitars."[1] In chapter 1 we used this video as an example of how viral content can negatively impact a company's reputation. Here we want to go a little deeper and explore how content that *resonates* with people can be key in overcoming resistance to sharing something into their networks. Recall that David Carroll created his video after spending nine months seeking compensation from United Airlines after discovering that the neck of his $3,500 Taylor guitar had been broken in transit. According to Carroll, United's customer service responded with complete indifference to his claims, even though he and other passengers witnessed baggage handlers tossing guitars to each other. Up to this point, we could change the details of the story (guitar with skis, for example) and have themes that consumers are all too familiar with: large corporation espouses commitment to satisfied customers but utterly fails to deliver; large corporation avoids taking responsibility for its actions; large corporation cares more about bottom line than people. These themes are so universal in today's culture that it is far from a surprise when a friend shares a story of how some big company broke, lost, or misrepresented items, skimped on, or overcharged for services, or ignored, lost, or disregarded complaints. Most people give up the fight against the corporate, legal, and bureaucratic roadblocks. But Carroll didn't.

When Carroll and his band, "Sons of Maxwell," posted their video on YouTube, it *resonated* with people. They could relate to it. As bloggers posted links to the video, they received comments like, "It's musical, it's funny, it wears well, and it really hits a raw spot,"[2] ". . . think back to the last time an airline lost your luggage, or damaged it, or just plain didn't care."[3] Researchers studying Twitter have found that content that *resonates* with users is more likely to grow into a viral trending topic than content that does not (Asur et al. 2011).

However, you can find thousands of YouTube videos that are effectively public-soap-box customer complaints that few people watch. The United video isn't just about resonance. The video is funny and has high production quality as well. Researchers have found that humor is certainly one of the elements that can help content go viral (Kirby and Marsden 2012; Shifman and Blondheim 2010). Good content certainly helps as well. Researchers (Petrovic et al. 2011; Suh et al. 2010) studying tweets that went viral found that the richness of the tweet (i.e., hashtags, urls @mentions) and even novelty were all related to the likelihood of tweets being retweeted. Have you ever given up listening to your favorite song on the radio because of static? The static can be so distracting that you can't focus on the song. Poor presentation of your message, whether we are talking about a tweet, a video, a post on a blog or

Facebook, can cost you members of an audience who might otherwise pay attention to you. And each person who stops reading or stops watching means one less person who might forward the content and push the message toward a critical point.

This doesn't mean that production quality must be high for something to go viral. Far from it. During the London Riots in the summer of 2011, people uploaded thousands of videos, many of which were jerky with poor light and sound.[4] Likewise, in the winter of 2010 hundreds of Seattle residents uploaded videos of cars sliding out of control on the steep city streets that were covered with ice.[5] In terms of virality, what these videos lacked in production quality they made up for in terms of *context*. The London and Seattle videos were important to many of the people that watched them right when they were happening. They were *salient*. Salience is when something is important in the moment, and is in part being in context for those consuming content. Research on the spread of memes (Knobel and Lankshear 2007) suggests that people's susceptibility to spreading messages depends, in part, on its salience in their lives. Also, Allsop et al. (2007: 402) claim that one principle behind people passing on messages is that it "happens in the context of a specific situation and occasion."

To understand how salience and context can work in supporting or hindering a viral spread, let's consider content about Sarah Palin, former Governor of Alaska and John McCain's Republican running mate in the 2008 U.S. Presidential election. Nearly any video about Sarah Palin would have gone viral the day John McCain announced her as his choice for Vice President. The context was: (1) the 2008 U.S. Presidential election, which many considered a high-stakes election due to the troubled economy; (2) as McCain pulled ahead of other possible Republican nominees, speculation about his choice of running mate grew; (3) Palin was a relative unknown outside of Alaska and people were hungry for information about her. A video made about her today, without some sort of scandal to drive interest, could still go viral, but without the context, she would not be perceived as salient in people's lives. Of course, what is salient to one person may not be salient to others. Since we are writing a book about virality, we may seek out some of the more humorous viral videos about Palin. For us, today, she is salient. But if we share the videos with our friends, they are unlikely to spread them; unless they are specifically *interested* in Sarah Palin or videos of the 2008 Presidential election.

Interest networks

In the last section, we focused on what made content remarkable to people. One set of these factors was information characteristics (novelty, resonance, quality, and humor). Another important information characteristic related to viral events is the interest around the topic of content that connects people together. Researchers have found that interesting content, as rated by study participants, is certainly one factor in whether or not people will share links (Bakshy et al. 2011). Recall that in chapter 2 we said that viral events can facilitate the creation of *interest networks, temporally bound, self-organized networks where membership is based on an interest in the information content or an interest in being included in the interest network of others.* What this means is that a viral event may emerge out of people sharing content that is *interesting* to them even if the content doesn't have high production value, isn't funny, doesn't resonate with them, and doesn't leave them with positive emotional feelings.

In fact, Ravikant and Rifkin (2010) argue that Twitter is essentially one large interest network organized around topics of interest more than social connection. These interest networks can also arise out of interactions on recommendation systems (Leskovec et al. 2006), blogs (Schmidt 2007), and content sharing sites like Flickr (Herrema 2011). Just within the last few years, the (pardon the overuse) interest in interest networks has grown as marketers seek to exploit our social networks in an effort to compete for our attention. Indeed, in an effort to target potential customers, marketing researchers develop algorithms aimed at identifying groups in networks who share interests (Leskovec et al. 2006). Beyond the commercial perspective, interest networks can help us identify people with whom we share passions and they can help activists find supporters, and will likely become fodder for research in sociology, political science, information science, and other fields in the coming years.

How do interest networks work? Many of us are passionately interested in topics that the people we are close to are indifferent about. Here is an example. Jeff is a passionate R programmer. According to the R website, "R is a free software environment for statistical computing and graphics."[6] He enjoys solving math and programming problems that allow him to make visualizations of data, particularly social networks. While most of the people he is close to think the visualizations are aesthetically appealing, none of them are interested in how they are made. But some people are interested.

We'll use a video[7] that Jeff posted on YouTube to explore interest networks a little further. In 2012 Jeff made an animation of a Twitter network. The links faded out over time, which was a new way of visualizing dynamic social networks. Frankly, the animation won't hold most people's attention for the entire two minutes, and most people that ran across the link would not click on it, unless they had a very specific set of overlapping or related interests. Since R is used in so many different kinds of analysis – everything from biostatistics, data analytics, finance, general statistics, and even analyzing speech patterns – we would expect a relatively small subset of them to be interested in network analysis, and an even smaller subset to want to watch an animation of a dynamic social network. While Jeff is a dedicated R programmer, he knows few people in the broader community who share his interests in network animation, so when his video went viral he was quite surprised. To be more exact, a "how to" blog post he wrote, with the video embedded as an example, went viral in the R community, which caused the video to go viral and get shared into groups that had an interest in the content.

Here's how it happened. Jeff wrote the blog post with the video and detailed instructions so that other R users could create their own network animation. He submitted the post to R-bloggers,[8] a well-known blog about R programming. In the R community, R-bloggers is a *hub* in that it connects R users who read and write about using R. The visitor traffic for R-bloggers is roughly 10,000 visitors a day, substantially higher than the traffic for SoMeLab.net, where Jeff posted the article. R-bloggers in this context acts as a network gatekeeper in that it connects users and networks who wouldn't otherwise be connected. Jeff's video went viral within the R community, an interest network.

Recall that in chapter 2 we said that the concept of virality was scalable, so a few hundred views could qualify as viral if the process by which it spread fit the criteria of reaching a critical mass within the interested community and being shared socially. If no one shared the video and all the views came from people who watched the embedded video on R-bloggers, we would call this a kind of broadcast. But people did share it. Using YouTube analytics, we found that 52 percent of the views came from the R-bloggers site and 13 percent came from SoMeLab.net, with Google,[9] Facebook, Reddit, and Twitter making up 27 percent of views, and the remaining views coming from YouTube sources.[10] Using sites like Bitly.com and Topsy.com, we were able find tweets and other social media shares where users had posted or tweeted a link to the video into their own networks, and in some cases retweeted or reshared these links. For example, we found traces of the video in topic areas such as data visualization groups and forums about general statistics. This is clearly beyond our expectation of a narrowly defined set of overlapping topics: network analysis and data animation. From our analysis, about a quarter of the views the video received came from social sharing of some sort. We also found that when two key R users, who had affiliations with other interest communities, shared the video, it spread into these other groups as well.

This highlights that when people find content remarkable in a topical area that they are interested in, a viral event may emerge as the content hops from network to network. We call this an interest network because it is based on a topic of interest along an ephemeral network constituted around a specific topic.

When we trace these networks, we see how people are connected through information diffusion. Since the network is based on the movement of content, once the content stops flowing, the network ceases to exist. However, the paths, or links, by which the content flowed, are often known or discoverable. This means people that are weakly connected, or not connected at all, may end up having conversations about the content. After Jeff's blog post and video went out, he answered several emails and comments on the blog. Some of these have led to conversations.

Thus, viral content can facilitate conversations, which, over time, can form more durable connections. The reach of viral events – their ability to hop from one network to another – means that people may be randomly exposed to ideas, information, and other content that otherwise might never have reached them. As a result, they may find that they unexpectedly share interests with people they know only casually, or they may find that there are existing communities who share the same interests they have. Repeatedly invoked interest networks, over time, may bring people together who, by discovering they share topics of mutual salience, may form more durable, influential, and actionable networks.

Just to summarize, here are the key characteristics of interest networks:

1. Since messages are forwarded from person to person, interest networks come into existence along the links that connect people who are interested in the same content.
2. These networks are ephemeral, meaning once the message ceases being forwarded, that specific interest network may no longer exist.
3. If many, topically similar viral events invoke interest networks with the same members, more durable connections may form.
4. These networks are bound by the collection of people who view the message, whether they reshare it or not.

The role of personal influence

At the beginning of this chapter we noted that we are focused on answering the question of why something goes viral from an individual perspective. To do so, we need to understand how people influence each other, which is a topic that marketers have long researched.[11] Key to their perspective is the idea that messages, which spread *organically* from one consumer to another, are more influential than advertising messages. More specifically, a great deal of research literature suggests that people are more likely to be influenced by people they know and to whom they have a personal connection (Allsop et al. 2007; Katz and Lazarsfeld 1955; Kiss and Bichler 2008; Watts and Dodds 2007). These people are typically referred to as opinion leaders.[12] Moreover, some people will have influence on us more than other people. In their work on the word-of-mouth (WOM) spread of product information, Allsop et al. (2007: 399) state that "not all social networks are equal, and not all individuals in a given social network have equal influence." This implies that we are more influential than some, and less than others. They also find that influential people tend to be influential in one or a few topic areas and not in others. For example, if you'd like a book recommendation for R programming, you might go along with Jeff's suggestions about which are worthwhile and which are not. However, Jeff's recommendations about which shoes go with which shirt are not as likely to influence people.

The research on opinion leaders comes largely from marketing, where the focus is on persuading people to purchase products. In other words, the researchers are interested in finding ways to get people to buy things they might not otherwise buy. They are interested in changing behaviors and the idea is that if a product recommendation comes from an expert, for example, you are more likely to be swayed. But diffusion of information and diffusion of behavior may work differently. In other words, the same people whom we might get important information from may not be the same people who influence our behavior, and the people who tend to influence our behavior may not be the people we get information from.

Research has shown that people we are close to are far more likely to influence our behavior (Bakshy et al. 2012; Barash et al. 2012; Brown and Reingen 1987; González-Bailón et al. 2011). Research has also shown that new ideas or novel information is more likely to come to us through people we do *not* know very well (Bakshy et al. 2012; Barabasi 2003; Burt 2004; Granovetter 1973, 1983; Walther et al. 2010). Since most of the content that goes viral is in the form of some kind of information, we think the people we are weakly connected to are more important in the spread of virality, though our close friends do play a role. If you think about all the people you know, you can quickly distinguish between people you are close to and people you might call acquaintances. Network researchers typically refer to the people we are close to as *strong ties*, and people that, for example, we knew from college that we occasionally talk to as *weak ties*. Of course in real life, these distinctions are far more nebulous. How we might rank people, in terms of closeness, changes over time as we become closer and move away from people. But the distinction is helpful for our discussion of how virality moves in social networks. As we explained in chapter 2, close friends help distribute information faster, but weak ties are better at spreading farther.

To make this a concrete example, let's suppose your spouse had sent you a link to David Caroll's "United Breaks Guitars" video when it first came out. You would be more likely to watch the video than if an old college friend that you communicated with infrequently sent you the same link. In other words, your spouse is more likely to influence your behavior, to get you to click on the link. On the other hand, the thinking goes, we typically already know about the things our close ties know about, so it is less likely that truly new information will come from them. This is because we tend to have similar interests and interact more often with those we are close to.

What this means for a video like "United Breaks Guitars" is that when someone wrote a blog post, or tweeted about it, their cluster of close friends are a bit more likely to go ahead and watch the video than the people that they are weakly tied too, but when one of these weakly linked people does watch the video, if they then repost it, they are bringing the content to their own cluster of strongly linked friends, who are a bit more likely to watch it since it came from a close tie in their own network. As we said in chapter 2, this is how viral content can hop, via weak links, from cluster to cluster, and once in the cluster, the strong ties influence behavior and get people to watch the video.

In our study of political blogs linking to viral videos in the U.S. 2008 Presidential election, we analyzed the content of the videos as well as the blog posts that linked to the videos and found that, by and large, bloggers tended to post links to videos when the message of the video matched the ideology of the blog. Social science has often referred to this tendency as homophily (Goodreau et al. 2009; Louch 2000; McPherson et al. 2001). The idea is that a set of homogeneous people along lines of socio-demographic and interpersonal characteristics such as race, marriage, friendship, gender, religion, age, class, and education are more likely to form relationships than heterogeneous people. Most of the literature about relationships in social media has exhibited similar trends of homophily (Bisgin et al. 2010; Lauw et al. 2010). People who are more similar are more likely to be interested in the same things. Returning to our study, we found that videos that praised Obama or bashed McCain were more likely to be linked to from liberal bloggers and, on the other side, conservative bloggers tended to link to videos where McCain was portrayed positively or Obama was bashed. There were cases where cross-ideological linking happened. This tended to be when the message of the video could be used to support an argument or interpreted favorably by the cross-linking blogger. For example, liberal bloggers linked to a few conservative videos and argued that the right was falling into using attack ads. This shows that once something goes viral, other opinion leaders can use the content, or spin the message in ways that were not originally intended (Nahon et al. 2013).

The question of whether people who are close influence each other's behavior, or whether they behave the same because they are similar and their similarity is why they are close, has not been resolved (Aral et al. 2009; Shalizi and Thomas 2011). People who are similar are more likely to form connections. But in a very popular book, Christakis and Fowler (2009) claimed that our eating habits are *influenced* by people up to three degrees away from us: you, your sibling, your sibling's friend, your sibling's friend's mother, whom you have never met! This is a behavior–influence chain, so the people involved – the ones directly connected – are strongly linked.[13]

Different types of people may wield different kinds of influence, which may affect virality in different ways. For example, Malcolm Gladwell (2002) introduced three types of opinion leaders, which he called connectors, mavens, and persuaders. Gladwell refers to these as personality types. Boster et al. (2011) have developed scales where they can measure the degree to which people have these qualities. We'll use ourselves as examples to illustrate each of these types.

People that spend any time with Karine quickly start saying "she knows everybody," so she is a connector and she is quick to introduce people who might otherwise not meet. In terms of information flows, she bridges groups of people. We've already noted that people consider Jeff an expert at R programming. As maven, in Gladwell's terms, he enjoys showing people how to do things with it, and when he sends out a link to a video or blog post about R, the people who know his work pay attention. Our publisher, John, certainly can be persuasive. He is charismatic and good at making a clear argument in a cheerful way so that people want to agree with him. When he introduces content to new people, he makes a compelling pitch for it. These should be considered ideal types, since very few people would embody a single one of them. According to Boster et al. (2011), very few people would be considered super-diffusers, scoring high on all measures.

Let's bring this back to virality. Let's say you make a video and you want it to go viral. Quality of content and other considerations aside, you are more likely to be able to get the people closest to you to watch it, either through similar interests or influence, than people a few links away. But to get it to spread, you still need an opinion leader of some sort. Research by Wu et al. (2011) shows that if you can get a celebrity to share your video it has the best chance of getting out to a large audience. Most of us don't know too many truly famous people, but we likely know people who are more influential than us in some way. The types of opinion leaders mentioned above can help think about where to try and promote it. If your video is technical, you might try and find a topic expert to help you bring the content to other groups. If your video is going to try and make a point about something, you might be best finding a persuasive sort of person to persuade people to watch the whole thing. They should be told it will be worth their while somehow. If you have a light video you just want to expose to many different groups, consider a connector who knows *everybody*. Instead of thinking of this as a recipe, think of it as a set of considerations.

Once you get your friends and a few opinion leaders to share your video, if it reaches a tipping-point, it can develop momentum. People start watching it because it is "hot" or because "everybody else has seen it." You can call this a bandwagon effect or an information cascade, which we mentioned in chapter 2. The idea is that if everyone else saw it, it must be worth seeing. Selecting hot content takes less work than finding new content and even has the added benefit of giving us something to talk to our friends about. In our study of political viral videos about the 2008 Presidential election, our results suggested that bloggers engaged in a bandwagon effect, posting links to videos simply because they were *hot*. This can create a positive feedback loop that feeds on itself until everyone who would engage with the content has and by then it is old news. But once something is trending, then sites like Twitter and YouTube feature it, which gives it more views.

Out of the complexity of the crowd emerges virality

The bottom-up perspective is a complex one. In it, content that is remarkable often has several qualities that, when combined, increase the likelihood that people will find the video worth remarking on. But different kinds of content will be of interest to some and not others depending on many factors, including context. We are more likely to be interested in. Content that people we are similar to are also interested in. But we are also more likely to be exposed to new content from the people we are only weakly connected too. Even when we are exposed to new and interesting content, the role of personal influence can be important in whether or not we share the content into our own networks, but those who are influential in one category are likely not influential in many other categories. If the content is on the cusp of being remarkable, the source – whom we received the link from – can be the deciding factor as to whether or not we share it into our own networks. Add to all of this factors like time of day, social context, and whether or not other content is competing for people's attention, which is almost always the case, and the picture is complex indeed. This is precisely why so few things go viral: the majority of content is just not simultaneously remarkable to enough people.

When *everything* lines up – the *right* content with the *right* source at the *right* time of day – then a viral event can emerge as a result of many people deciding something is remarkable, and then doing just that: remarking on, and sharing, some bit of content. We generally don't even think about how our individual sharing, when combined with hundreds, or thousands, or millions of other people's sharing, collectively creates a pattern of information flows that we call virality.

In the next chapter, we tie these two perspectives, top-down and bottom-up, together by focusing on the structures of the networks that we are embedded in. We show how our networks, our position in them and the ways we are connected, affect viral events. But chapter 5 is just the first part of our discussion about *structure*. In chapter 6 we will look at another type of structure, social structure, and explore how viral events affect these structures.

5

What Makes Something Viral III: Caught in the viral net!

This chapter completes the trilogy of chapters, addressing the question of *why* something becomes viral. In chapter 3 we focused on the top-down aspects of virality. In chapter 4 we shifted our attention and described the bottom-up aspects of virality, such as emotional aspects, context, and information characteristics. In this chapter we tie those together by discussing how the *structures of networks* impact virality, and to what degree virality is controllable.

Structures of networks: Flowing according to the rules of the games

The concept of *structure* has received many treatments from scholars in a variety of social science disciplines (Bourdieu 1977; Durkheim 1982; Foucault 1978, 1990; Giddens 1986; Weber 1946). It is beyond the scope of this book to delve deeply into the various conceptualizations of structure. For us, *structure of networks* encompasses two main aspects: first, the rules, practices, and arrangements through which the behavior of people is regulated[1] in networks, and second, it reflects "the typology of interconnected nodes" (Castells 2009) identified by "the observed set of ties linking the members of a population" (Watts 2004: 48) in their social networks.

Let's give some examples to make this clearer. Twitter constrains the number of characters in tweets to 140 characters. Designing Twitter in this way has major ramifications on the content that flows over its service. When users are bound to 140 characters, their posts must be short, laconic, and abbreviated in many cases. One would not start discussing the philosophy of Aristotle in Twitter with followers, but one might use it to alert followers about Hurricane Sandy approaching the United States' east coast. It is not a coincidence that Twitter is mainly used to report ongoing events that occur in real time. It was purposely structured this way by its designers, leveraging the simple message standard (SMS) protocol and consequently people use Twitter in similar ways to those they might use when texting messages: short reports of what they are doing in their present moment (Sagolla 2009). By implementing the service in this way, a 140-character limit, Twitter has created a structure that enables some behaviors and prohibits others.

Another example of structures in networks is the use of hashtags (#) in Twitter, which boyd et al. note are used "to mark tweets topically so that others can follow conversations centering on a particular topic" (boyd et al. 2010). Hashtags were not originally a Twitter design feature. Norms around their use arose out of the collective practices of users. Use of hashtags later spread to other platforms and are now in daily use. The hashtag is part of the structure of the network in that it functions as a classifier that allows other people to follow conversations. It is crucial in setting the boundaries of interest networks.

But network structure also refers to the shapes and patterns we see in the links connecting people in social networks. These links are dynamic and change in networks all the time as we meet new people or lose touch with old friends. As the connections between people change, the patterns in the networks also change. Many of the connections we make are limited to specific contexts, like people we interact with only at work, friends on Facebook that we haven't seen in person for a decade, or a favorite sibling who is happy to chat on the phone, but never logs on to her email or Facebook account. Of course, the kind of link, as well as the opportunity to link with specific people, is related to the links we already have and the rules and practices of the social system that we are embedded in. Our interest in network structures for the purpose of this book lies in their role in driving viral events.

Virality is a process of people sharing information with other people that happens over social networks. These networks form as a result of people making connections with one another. As we will show in this chapter, the network structure plays an important role in the flow of information, and thus the emergence and eventual magnitude of a viral event.

We have already introduced some structural patterns found in networks, for example, we discussed how information tends to flow easily in *clusters*, which we said were sub-networks of tightly connected people, and that *network holes* are the spaces between clusters where there are few links (see chapter 2). Network gatekeepers can be thought of as a structural aspect of networks too, because they are often in a position to span network holes and link together different clusters in a network. In this chapter we will cover three other aspects of network structures and their influence in viral events. These are, the power-law distribution of scale-free networks (a few people have many links while most people have comparatively few links); the effects of being closer to the *core* of a network; and the idea that our highly interconnected social networks are distributed, which means that in many cases people can link directly together without gatekeepers.

Power-law distribution: The attention-rich get richer

Instead of discussing these structural elements with a single viral case, or even a viral topic, we are going to look at a research project in which our lab studied 120 videos that went viral during the 2008 Presidential elections in the U.S. (Nahon and Hemsley 2011; Nahon et al. 2011). The 2008 election was characterized by a growing use of social networking sites, including video platforms, such as YouTube, which became important vehicles for mobilization by political elites and users (Castells 2009). By the end of the campaign, fully 60 percent of online political users had watched some sort of video related to the politics of the election, and political blogs served as important information venues for the public regarding the elections (26 percent of internet users) (Smith 2009). We were interested in understanding the role of blogs in driving viral processes.

We found that there were four types[2] of blogs that impacted viral videos differently:

1. *Elite blogs*, made up of just the Huffington Post and *Daily Kos*, two highly ranked and well-known political blogs that linked to many of the videos that went viral in our set.
2. *Top-political blogs*, the top 50 conservative and liberal blogs at the time.
3. *Top-general blogs*, blogs that were not primarily political in nature but were popular (based on the number of unique visitors per day, or *traffic*, in 2008).
4. *Tail blogs*, made up of all other blogs that linked to one of the videos in our set.

For figure 5.1 we sorted the blogs in our study by how many unique visitors they received on a given day in 2008 (*traffic*). Each blog's symbol represents which category it is in and the size of the symbol shows how many of our viral videos they linked too. The two largest symbols (triangles) represent the Huffington Post, at the top, with the Daily Kos below, but still with a significant amount of traffic. The top general blogs (diamonds), many of whom linked infrequently to our videos, are shown as generally having the next highest level of traffic, with the top-political blogs (stars) mixed in but generally lower than the top-blogs. Tail blogs

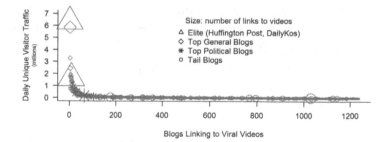

Figure 5.1: Power-law distribution of blogs by traffic.

(circles) have the lowest volume of traffic and stretch off to the right side of the graph.

The graph illustrates the idea of a power-law distribution[3] of links in a network because we can see that a few blogs were visited by millions of people every day, while the majority of blogs got only a few visitors a day. In this context, link does not necessarily mean a social connection, but rather, the link by which information flows from one person (a blogger) to another (the reader). It turns out that a power-law distribution of attention or linking is a pretty normal social pattern that we see both on- and offline: a few individuals get most of the attention while most of the people get significantly less. Of course, capturing the attention of others may later translate into the ability to influence people. On Twitter, people like Justin Bieber and Lady Gaga would be on the far left because they get so much attention, and Jeff and Karine would be farther to the right – much farther. In the tail.

In our study we found that each type of blog had a specific role in the life cycle of virality (see figure 5.2).

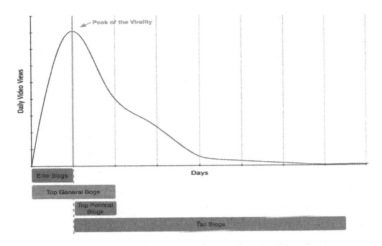

Figure 5.2: Viral life cycle of content in the blogosphere

In other words, their position in the structure of the network has an impact on their role in driving viral events. Each type of blog tended to post links to videos at different times and thus impacted the signature of virality in different ways. The elite blogs and top general blogs appeared to ignite viral events by posting links to videos early and thus bringing those videos to the attention of hundreds of thousands of people, sometimes millions. When that happened, some of those people shared it into their own networks (via blogs, Facebook, Twitter, or email) in the familiar pattern of a viral spread. Drezner and Farrell's (2008) work suggests that not only do these blogs capture the attention of a majority of readers, but also that mainstream media elites and other bloggers also follow these blogs.

At the core of things

The data set we used included over 10,000 blogs, linking to the 120 videos in our set, so the findings are about the overall temporal patterns of viral events, and not about the exact path of sharing for each viral event. We mention this because the group of top political blogs holds an important position in the network: they are situated in or near the *core*. For this discussion, we can think of the core of a network as a set of people who are highly interconnected, but as a group they are also well connected throughout the network.[4] Since we are concerned with viral events that flow across media platforms, the actors in the network core tend to be people or organizations who are gatekeepers, or actors close to gatekeepers. As a structural concept, the core matters because people near the core of a network tend to be more influential in spreading messages than people with the same number of links but farther from the core (Kitsak et al. 2010). As an example, let's imagine a blogger who gets about 100 visitors a day, but all of those visitors are friends who write at immensely popular blogs in the core of the network. Our imagined blogger is in, or close to, the core because of her direct connections with other core bloggers even though she doesn't have many links. But she is also more likely to get the attention of these other core bloggers than someone with the same number of links, or even more, who is not read at all by the core bloggers.

When we consider this idea of core influence alongside Drezner and Farrell's (2008) suggestion that top-blogs scan the blogosphere and highlight important information by reposting it, an interesting picture emerges. In this view, Huffington Post is in the core of the network because they have many connections and are connected to other bloggers who are also well connected.[5] When a blogger at Huffington Post finds a link to an interesting video, it will more likely be at some top-political blog that is in or near the core than at one of the hundreds of thousands of tail blogs. This is because these core/near-core blogs are interconnected with each other. In support of this, Wu et al. (2011) found that categories of elite Twitter users (e.g., celebrities, media outlets, and bloggers) tended to pay attention to other users from their own categories more than users from different categories. Content that is promoted at the mid-range of the power-law, or closer to the core of the network, can work its way up. This pattern of blogs, at a higher level, finding content from smaller blogs and promoting it, is replicated at the mid-range/tail of the power-law as well. In other words, the top-political blogs may find content in the tail and promote it up, which may again get promoted up. In this way, content can *bubble up*. The bubble-up process can happen very quickly because professional bloggers are always on the lookout for new content to post.

Once a blog like Huffington Post links to a video, other blogs that follow it (core and tail) will see the video and may post to it as well. So while content can bubble up, it can also flow down to many smaller blogs and reach both a large audience and deep into networks. Likewise, if a video makes it up to a top-political blog, but not up to Huffington Post, other top-political blogs and the tail blogs that follow them may link to the video as well. This *bubble-up* and *downward flow* representation helps explain why we see the signatures of viral events (see figures 5.1 and 2.4) decay over a longer period of time than the amount of time it takes for them to take off. It also helps us understand how viral events can be thought of as *scalable*. A blog like Huffington Post needs to post content that appeals to a broad audience, so a library video, like the Lady Gaga video from chapter 2, may not get picked up by Huffington Post, but if it bubbled up to bloggers who are *core* to the library community, then they might repost it and start a large downward flow of linking to the video within the library community. The library video would reach many people in the library community, but not such a massive audience as a link from Huffington Post could generate, but would still be considered viral.

Up to this section of the book we have been talking about viral events flowing on a particular social network like Facebook or Twitter, but we can see from this example that blogs also share content and stories, and that when they link to a YouTube video or a story on another site, they connect two or more different platforms. When many blogs link to a video at the same time, we can have many-to-many sharing as we do in social networking sites. Also, people on Facebook and Twitter read blogs and reshare content they find there into their own networks. Thus, the viral process can spread within and across multiple social media platforms at the same time.

Before we leave our discussion about the power-law distribution of links, and thus attention, we want to note that a key takeaway is that where someone is situated on

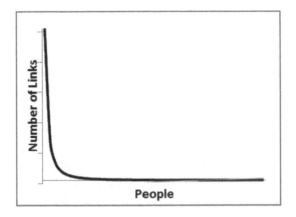

Figure 5.3: Example of a power-law

the power-law graph is directly related to the likelihood that the content they share or reshare reaches a large audience. Figure 5.3 exemplifies a power-law distribution (see note 10 in chapter 2) where a small number of people is being linked to by the majority of people within the network. This works in two ways. First, people on the far left of the graph have many links and represent a higher level of power in terms of their ability to reach a large audience and span multiple networks, thus causing a downward flow of sharing; and second, the farther to the left they are, the more likely they are to have links to people who have even more links then they do, who can then spread the content even farther. Barabasi (2003) calls networks with this kind of power-law configuration a *scale-free* network, or the 'rich get richer' syndrome in terms of links. Stated differently, the closer content gets to the core of a network, the more likely it is to be picked up and reshared by media elites.

The last aspect of scale-free networks to discuss is called the *clustering coefficient*.[6] The farther to the right (fewer ties) on the power-law graph you are, the more likely you are to be in a dense cluster (higher coefficient) where everyone knows everyone else and many of your connections are strong ties. But this also means that the farther to the left you are (more ties), the more likely it is that only a tiny fraction of your ties are strong ties. Of course, if we took two people, one from the far left and one from the far right, they could both have the same number of strong ties, say 10, but the person from the left side of the graph could have thousands of times more weak links than the person from the right side of the graph.

This is important for information diffusion because a great deal of research shows that individuals are more likely to receive new information from weak ties than from strong ties (Bakshy et al. 2012; Barabasi 2003; Burt 2004; Granovetter 1973, 1983; Rogers 2003; Walther et al. 2010). So people farther to the left not only have far more connections, they are also more likely to have more sources of *new* information than those farther to the right. If your livelihood as a blogger depends on finding and posting links to new and interesting content, then having more weak ties gives you an advantage over those with fewer weak ties.[7] In other words, a person from the left side would be able to reach out to a larger number of people, and potentially also reach to farther networks than a person on the right. And the opposite is also true. The person on the left side would be able to get newer information due to their larger number of weak ties.

Because people on the right side of the power-law graph have fewer weak ties, they are less likely to have connections to people in far-off clusters. But research has also shown that messages spread more easily in these strong tie clusters, but need weak heterophily links to span network holes (the space between clusters) and reach farther out into the wider network (Barabasi 2003; Burt 2004; Rogers 2003; Walther et al. 2010). In other words, information will spread faster in a network through people who are closer to us, but will need people that are less close to spread farther. Huberman and Adamic (2004) have even shown that message diffusion in a scale-free network has a threshold related to the distance between nodes. This means that without people who can span the holes in networks with their many weak ties, viral events would generally remain small if they happened at all.

It is important to note that sometimes this may not hold true. The social infrastructure we share content on is made up of platforms that are designed to support distributed networks (Barabasi 2003; Benkler 2006; Galloway 2004). A distributed network is one where there are many paths connecting any two people. So people in the tail who generally count on gatekeepers to connect their clusters are still connected via multiple pathways, but the content may have to pass through more people to get from person A to person B. This is how viral events can circumvent gatekeepers and how grass-roots viral events start: they become popular in small clusters and hop from one to another until so many people know about it that they start asking why the traditional media haven't covered the story yet.

Bottom-up emergence vs. top-down control

Where does the content come from that these blogs are directing so much attention to, and thus acting as key drivers in the viral process? Virality is a mix of top-down and bottom-up factors where people exchange information. As an example, Broxton et al. (2010) note that the number of views a viral video receives is not entirely the result of a social exchange process. Features on social media platforms may direct users' attention to content to which they would not otherwise have been exposed. On YouTube, people are shown related videos in a side bar, and Twitter shows trending topics on its main page. Additionally, topics that are trending, or videos that go viral, like "United Breaks Guitars," are increasingly becoming fodder for mainstream media stories, drawing even more attention to the original content. Thus not all of the attention viral events receive is a result of a many-to-many mass-self communication social process. In fact, the overwhelmingly majority of viral items are derivatives, responses, or copies of content generated by the mass-media producers (Asur et al. 2011; Burgess and Green 2009; Crane and Sornette 2008; Kwak et al. 2010). On the other hand, recent work by Wu et al. (2011) has shown that while traditional media sources tend to be among the most active users on Twitter, only about 15 percent of tweets that ordinary users receive are from them. They also note that about 20,000 elite users attract about 50 percent of the attention (measured by the spread of URLs) on Twitter, but that the bulk of the remaining content shared on Twitter is from ordinary users. Similarly, studying information flows on

Twitter, Yang and Leskovec (2010) found that people with a low number of followers were nearly as likely to *start* a viral event as those with many followers, but that largest viral events tended to have been retweeted by people with a large number of followers. This supports the idea that while a great deal of viral content can come from the mainstream media, either as direct content or as a mash-up, bubbling up of viral events does happen.

So what is the *right* mix of top-down and bottom-up forces? How much is the process controllable? Viral events are ubiquitous. However, such events constitute only a small percentage of social media content. A vast majority of YouTube videos receive few views (Crane and Sornette 2008), and only a small percentage of tweets are retweeted (boyd et al. 2010; Hemsley and Mason 2012). Nevertheless, the role of viral events in society is of great magnitude. From chapters 1 and 2 we covered viral signatures, which can help us identify viral events, and noted that human social sharing that spreads quickly and reaches far – in terms of both total audience and links traveled – is a defining element of virality. In our research and the work of others, we have found patterns in viral events, such as the crucial role of network gatekeepers, which we covered in chapter 3. In chapter 4, we highlighted some of the elements of viral content that make it remarkable, such as emotional impact, resonance, salience, and interest. We also discussed the role of personal influence and noted that interest networks can form around the social sharing of viral content. This chapter was devoted to examining how the structures of social networks, such as the power-law distribution of attention/links and strong and weak ties, affect the flow of viral events.

If we ended the book here some readers might think that the viral process is controllable and that with the right recipe anyone can create viral events. We think not. As we have seen in many examples throughout this book, once content is posted in the public sphere, it is no longer controllable by those who post it. Content that we create can remain stubbornly obscure even when we apply our best efforts to promote it. It can also grow and spread with an apparent life and momentum of its own, destroying some people's lives and bringing fame and fortune to others, sometimes in a matter of days.

Even if something does go viral, the intended message is not assured. Marketers recognize that people "can be idiosyncratic, creative, and even resistant" (Kozinets et al. 2010: 73) to messages inserted into their networks. In their book, Kirby and Marsden note that the Carlsberg Beer Company was an early adopter of viral marketing campaigns and in 2004 experimented with a viral email campaign. Unfortunately, it went horribly wrong when someone added text in the email message that said "Shame their lager tastes like p*ss" (2012: 93), which was forwarded by recipients as if it was the real message. Even the meaning of videos can be altered. Those who share links can include text that frames in a certain way (Scheufele and Tewksbury 2007), or those who copy and repost videos can add annotations that also alter the meaning of the message.

We do think that content producers who are able to line up the right elements (e.g., willing gatekeepers for an interested targeted audience, high production quality, a message that is salient and resonates with people or has emotional impact) have a higher likelihood of their content going viral. But we also think that the degree to which content goes viral depends on many factors: for example, on the connectedness and audience sizes of all the actors who share or reshare that content. The complexity of the social behavior and overlapping contexts needed for something to go viral makes virality difficult to predict and control.

For us, the uncontrollable nature of virality makes the story of virality fascinating. Humans will probably continue to exploit it, and will continue trying to control the process. We think that, in general, marketers will get better at it, but that there will always be a degree of uncertainty in the process. Now that we have uncovered in the first part of the book the main elements of the black box of virality, we will move to analyze the effects it has on individuals, societies, and institutions.

6

Networked Changed Societies

Virality emerges as a result of a social process. As such it has a tremendous impact on individuals, collectives, and institutions. Viral events are ubiquitous, and yet they make up only a small percentage of social media content. The vast majority of YouTube videos receive few views (Crane and Sornette 2008), and only a small percentage of tweets are retweeted (boyd et al. 2010). In the sea of content, viral events emerge as something that stands apart. They are *remarkable*. By this we mean that they exhibit qualities such that people want to make a *remark* about them (as we addressed in chapter 4). People see in these events something that is worth sharing with their friends and followers. If enough people find the content remarkable and share it, they are collectively participating in the creation of a viral event. A great many viral events consist of newly released music videos, hot movie trailers, and even commercials (Burgess and Green 2009). But not all of them. Regardless of the video's content, viral events play an important role in modern society. In this chapter we examine the ways that virality affects society from three angles: the impact on the subject of the viral message (people or organizations), the impact on social structures as a result of participation in the viral process, and the impact of virality on institutions.

The perils and promises of virality

One cannot understand the extent of influence that virality has on our lives without understanding both the promises and threats embedded in a viral spread. On any given day, individuals, companies, and governments produce and promote content in an attempt to exploit virality in the hope that it will gain the attention of the public and reach the minds of millions of people. From the point of view of those trying to exploit it, virality contains the promise of exposure to many eyeballs with the possibility of influencing minds. For companies, this often means publicizing a brand name in ways that rouse positive feelings in viewers. As an example, Old Spice, a Proctor and Gamble subsidiary that makes men's deodorant, antiperspirant, and fragrances, posted a video on YouTube titled "Old Spice I The Man Your Man Could Smell Like."[1] In it, a shirtless Isaiah Mustafa, a fit and attractive male actor, quickly transitions from taking a shower to sailing a yacht to riding a horse on a beach, all while maintaining perfect eye contact and a relaxed demeanor and extolling the virtues of the Old Spice product. The playful video is 33 seconds long and has been viewed over 44 million times in the nearly three years since it was posted. This works out to more than 46 *years* of free advertising.

Another of virality's promises is its ability to communicate ideas. The reach by numbers and networks, which defines virality, is at the same time its mechanism, and its potential to impact individuals is its strength. Established in 2006, TED.com exemplifies this promise. TED, which stands for Technology, Entertainment, and Design, is a website and conference dedicated to disseminating "ideas worth spreading" ("TED: Ideas Worth Spreading" 2012). The main vehicle of dissemination is its online video channel, consisting of nearly 1,450 lectures at the time of this writing, which have attracted collectively over 1 billion views, often in a viral process. The popularity of the TED website appears to be viral itself, judging by its growth over the past five years (see figure 6.1).[2] Since the majority of videos are presentations of less than 20 minutes, given by practiced speakers on engaging topics, the videos are easy to digest and accessible to the general public. Each one of these talks has the potential to impact individuals and start a chain reaction: by simply increasing awareness of provocative and critical topics, and suggesting alternative ways of thinking about them, the actions and opinions of individuals may change. TED is perceived by many as a viral platform with which to disseminate ideas. This reputation itself may act as a driver, which may propel people to watch, regardless of the content.

Virality serves as a platform to spread ideas, innovations, communal information, or entertainment tidbits. Coursera is another example of an organization with growth driven by viral processes (email interview with

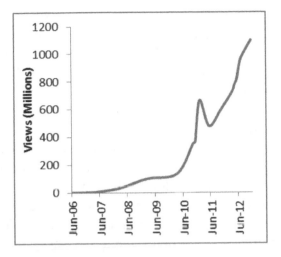

Figure 6.1: TED talks views

Daphne Koller, Coursera founder, December 6, 2012).[3] Where TED is a non-profit organization, Coursera is a for-profit educational technology company and may be at the forefront of a revolution in the field of education. Traditionally, universities and colleges have had a monopoly on issuing certificates and providing higher education. Coursera and other massive open online courses (MOOCs) offer university-level courses taught by professors online, in which the general public can enroll without being a matriculated student. These courses offer people the chance to acquire knowledge in ways never before possible. Certificates are given for completing courses and grading is done on the basis of peer-review from other students, making it possible for an instructor with a limited staff to manage very large courses. In terms of impact, Coursera offers about 157 courses to over 2 million students across more than 196 countries. TED and Coursera growth shows, first, that the viral process isn't exclusive to individual items of content and news about an organization; an idea and even an event can go viral. Second, when an idea or organization is remarkable enough to capture global attention, the potential for swift societal change is present.

But virality also poses a tremendous threat for individuals, companies, and governments. In chapter 1 we noted that Alexandra Wallace, a student at UCLA, received death threats after she posted a racist video on YouTube complaining about Asian students in the library. Wallace quickly removed her video from YouTube, but by then copies had been made and reposted, some of which also went viral. This illustrates that once viral content is posted in the public sphere, it is no longer controllable by those who post it. Of course viral events are not confined to truthful and good content. People can also create and post malicious content. In July 2010, conservative blogger Andrew Breitbart edited and posted a video of Shirley Sherrod, a high-ranking official in the U.S. Department of Agriculture. Breitbart's edits made it appear that Mrs. Sherrod admitted to discrimination against white farmers (Stelter 2010) and she was quickly forced to resign after the video went viral. Within a day, the original 1986 version of Sherrod's speech surfaced, showing her comments in context and making it clear that Breitbart's edits were deceptive and clearly intended to cast Sherrod in a negative light.[4] But by then the damage had been done: Shirley Sherrod's life had been disrupted even if her name had been cleared.

The Sherrod case was a smear campaign, but virality and its ecosystem (e.g., comments or memes about the content, additional content about the subject) have also been known to bring to light scandalous behavior of public officials. The sex scandal of General David Petraeus, Director of the Central Intelligence Agency, is one such case. His affair with Paula Broadwell, the author of Petraeus' biography, quickly became a viral topic. The news spread quickly through social media and mainstream media as photos of General Petraeus with his wife and with Ms. Broadwell surfaced. General Petraeus resigned from his duty on November 9, one day after the 2012 U.S. Presidential election and just one day after the affair was exposed. Of course, the consequences didn't end with the individuals at the center of this viral event. Both the affair and General Petraeus' resignation had national security and political implications for the U.S. The Obama administration was faced with appointing and ultimately confirming a new CIA director.

From the different examples above, there are a few key points worth mentioning. First, virality promises marketers, activists, organizations, and performers an audience limited only by how far a viral event extends into networks. This means that their products, grievances, ideas, and performances can reach fertile ground and blossom. Second, viral events can spread ill-intentioned and deceptive content as easily as scandalous and humorous content. Virality's speed means people's lives, careers, and social statuses can all be compromised in a matter of days or hours. In fact, the extent, speed, and sociability of virality correspond to a higher degree of perils and promises. This is also what makes virality distinct from other types of information flows in networks. Lastly, any single viral event can be a promise to one and, at the same time, a peril to another.

Virality's role in reproduction and transformation of social structure

This section discusses how virality impacts social structures. We define *social structure* in a similar way to how we defined *structure of networks* in chapter 5. For us, *social structure* encompasses two main aspects: first, the norms, rules, practices, and arrangements through which the behavior of people is regulated in societies, and second, at the same time its reflection of the structure of institutions that are part of the fabric of society (Thompson 1984). In this section we focus mainly on the first perspective of social structure, and in the next section we will talk about the structure of institutions.

Viral events are a mechanism of reproduction and transformation of social structures. In other words, they reproduce and transform norms, rules, practices, and arrangements that regulate our behavior. Social reproduction and transformation are ongoing processes that happen over the course of social interactions. At its most basic, social reproduction is the idea that each time we act in a way that is in line with the social norms of our group (or community, school, nation, etc.), we are reproducing those norms, and when we act in ways that are not accepted as normal, there is the potential for social transformation. As an example, let's suppose that we are part of a community with a specific dress code for its members. One day a young woman starts wearing blue jeans instead of the traditional garments. We might find that everyone shuns the casual dresser, or is even hostile towards her, either until she begins dressing more traditionally or until she stops being an active member in the community. As long as everyone is acting out the same patterns (wearing traditional garments and shunning those who do not), the norms are reproduced. But what if our casual dresser persists? At some point, other people might start accepting, or at least stop actively shunning, her. Eventually others might even think, "Hey, nothing bad happened to her, and I'm in a hurry, so just for today I'll wear jeans too." Slowly, over time, we might start seeing and accepting casually dressed members in the community. Through her persistent actions, the young woman in our example instigated a slow transformation of the norms of appropriate communal attire. Of course, it is far more complex in real social situations. The field of sociology is rich with different theoretical perspectives about what social structures are, how they come about and how people affect and are affected by them (Bourdieu 1984; Foucault 1990). As a framework for understanding how viral events can both reproduce and transform social structures, we draw on two well-established concepts. The first, *habitus*, as developed by the French sociologist Pierre Bourdieu (1977, 1990), will help us understand how virality can reproduce social structures. Then, we will use Anthony Giddens' structuration theory (1986) as our second theoretical lens to help us explore how viral events can transform social structures.

As Swartz notes, the complexity of Bourdieu's work makes summarizing a concept like habitus difficult, but we will start with the idea that habitus is what *regulates* our daily actions (Swartz 1997). For our purposes, the word regulate can entail *our regular actions* as well as the *disposition*, or propensity we have to act in one way and not another. Bourdieu sees actions as strategic, in that people make decisions to achieve objectives, but he also claims that our learned behaviors and expectations form the structures that regulate our practices that constitute social life (Swartz 1997). So, going back to our example of wearing traditional clothes, if one were to be raised in that community since childhood and observed everyone dressed in traditional garb, then as that child grew older, he/she would have a propensity to also dress traditionally. It would be *ir*regular not to dress according to the community dress code. If you have ever shown up at a party and felt under- or over-dressed, then you have an idea of what this means. But habitus also informs what we believe is appropriate and inappropriate, as well as possible and impossible for us; it shapes the choices we make without our being aware of it because we already have a propensity to behave one way over another. The child is socialized into the *practice* of dressing traditionally in public as a result of witnessing and participating in the act of being part of the community and may not even consider the option of wearing jeans.[5]

So how does virality reproduce social structures? Virality is a mechanism that can perpetuate common cultural narratives that reaffirm people's dispositions and practices. It does this through the viral content as well as the way in which the message spreads. We'll use an incredibly popular viral video to illustrate how this works. At the time of this writing, *Gangnam Style*,[6] the music video by the South Korean singer PSY, whose real name is Park Jae-Sang, has already been seen over one billion times. Many casual viewers will see the visuals in *Gangnam Style* as portraying women as secondary and valued for their sex appeal. In this light, it can be seen as reproducing the patriarchal values of a society where males are more powerful than women by showing relatively scantily clad women attending to an individual man. The women seem to have no role in the video other than as available sex objects. So, viewers of the video see social patriarchal values played out, as they would expect. Because the viral process involves social sharing, in which people are exposed to content that their friends share, there is a tacit association of the values and behaviors in the video with those who spread the content. Obviously this may be a kind of false legitimization of the message, as people can reshare content for many reasons, and as receivers of the message, we may or may not be aware of that. Additionally, the speed of virality, particularly in tight-knit clusters, implies that people can share a common cultural experience by not only viewing the video simultaneously, but also by discussing it afterwards. Thus, virality can serve as a mechanism of social structure reproduction through the social sharing of content, which works on three different levels.

First, the narratives of the content manifest the latent values and norms of the community. This provides members of the community with stories they can relate to, imitate, and even use as guidance for actions deemed appropriate. There are millions of latent gestures that are transmitted to us when we see such a video, and while we are generally not aware of it, the effect creates a latent enculturation process for each of us. This process socializes us into the culture and teaches us the correct behavior. Second, the sharing process itself can act as a tacit endorsement of the embedded values and norms. Third, the shared experience provides a common cultural experience, which can reinforce the norms and values as individuals discuss the experience. More to the point, viral events can reaffirm the way we think the world *should* look like, how people *should* dress, talk, laugh, and communicate in social situations.

The *Gangnam Style* video reproduces norms by modeling behavior, dress, and social interactions. By looking at the content of the video more deeply, we can also see how viral events can transform social structures. First, we need to briefly introduce Giddens' concept of structuration (1986), which we also use in the next section dealing with viral events and social institutions. For Giddens, the ways people are connected and organized make up the social *system*, while the *rules*, or, for our purposes, the norms that regulate people's behavior, comprise the social structure.[7] But, similar to Bourdieu, it is through our actions that the norms, and thus the structure, are created. When people's actions are in accordance with existing norms, they are effectively reproducing the social structure. However, when people's behavior deviates from the norms, slippages in the rules occur. Over time, these slippages can result in new norms, or a transformation of social structures.

The process of the reproduction and transformation of structure is called structuration and captures what Giddens saw as the dual nature of people's action and the social structure; for him, they are the same thing seen from different perspectives.

Now, let's look at PSY more deeply. *Gangnam Style* is actually being hailed as a subversive parody of South Korea's growing materialism, where personal debt is sky-high, people skimp on necessities so they can be seen purchasing expensive coffee, and the conspicuous consumption of those in the exclusive neighborhood known as "Gangnam" is seen as a model to be emulated (Fisher 2012; Onsemiro 2012). Juxtaposed with PSY's glitzy look and confidence are the locations of the scenes, which take place in playgrounds, busses, and parking lots instead of beaches, night clubs, and expensive hotels. Also, when PSY sees the object of his desire (Kim Hyun-a, a Korean pop star in her own right), he looks at her longingly instead of with the objectification we might expect. Of course, PSY's subtlety is lost on most Westerners who are unfamiliar with South Korea's culture. In the West, social critique in music is so common that subtlety is not needed. But in Korea it is. Instead of being familiar with the embedded sexist norms, the video's message is a challenge to materialist norms and the popular music culture, where music videos are generally quite tame, particularly with respect to being critical of society.

A key way this video might transform norms is through its massive viral success: Now that one critical music video has become massively successful, other musicians will certainly attempt to emulate PSY's style.

Over time, PSY's work, along with other artists', may create a climate of receptivity for cultural critique. A more direct way the video may transform norms is through the Korean public's awareness of the subtle message of the video: that materialism and conspicuous consumption are shallow and a farce. Only time will tell, but we may find that fans of PSY begin emulating his apparent disdain for such a materialist lifestyle.

Before we leave this topic, we wish to go through one more example of how viral events can transform social structures. On November 18, 2011, students from UC Davis gathered in the quad of the university, as part of the Occupy Wall Street movement, to demonstrate against ongoing tuition hikes and police violence. UC Davis police ordered the demonstrators to disperse, but the students remained seated and a crowd of onlookers chanted their support. At this point, two UC Davis police officers pepper-sprayed the line of seated protesters. The students were unarmed and posed no physical threat to the officers. They stayed seated, with their arms locked while Lieutenant John Pike causally walked up and down the line spraying the students. Members of crowd decried the action, all the while taking pictures and videos with their smartphones. These images and videos flooded social networks and the web. Many went viral. According to Scott (2011), news of the incident was aired on TV only after multiple videos of the event went viral.

The incident was not composed of one viral event, but many viral and non-viral streams of shared content, which, together, formed a viral topic. The topic was made up of videos, photos, blog posts, news articles, and memes. Each new shared message formed part of a larger discussion about the pepper spray incident. Most of the voices portrayed John Pike as a heartless, cruel person, exploiting his formal power as a police officer to trash the rights of people trying to make their voices heard through peaceful means (ACLU 2012). The viral topic itself became a symbol of people's outrage over the breaching of the demonstrators' rights and the brutality of the police. By sharing and forwarding content to friends, people were making a statement, consciously or unconsciously, that the right to protest peacefully ought to be protected, and that police brutality should not be tolerated. By making such a statement, they were both reproducing our value of free speech and transforming the norms of campus police by making clear what is and isn't acceptable behavior. Thus, the impact of virality is complex and can be seen as a duality, both reproducing and transforming social structure.

Virality can be helpful in countering ruling practices by suggesting alternative ways of thinking and conceptualizing social structure. The fact that hundreds of people took photos and video clips of the UC Davis officer reflects a change in the practices of citizens in that they can now document and share events in real time. Citizen documentation and real-time sharing may be new modes of civic participation. As their shared content goes viral, it draws the attention of a greater part of the public, who may also participate in the viral conversation. This may further encourage others to digitally speak out and participate in public discussions

111

with people both near and far; a transformation in the behavior and attitudes of people themselves, and perhaps a challenge to existing conceptions of what it means to engage in civil participation.

It also reflects a change in social structures where, through their actions of social sharing, citizens promote the values of transparency and accountability. There is a growing awareness that, as a group, citizens have the right and power to demand accountability: public servants must explain and take responsibility for their actions. In this way, virality may be one of the keys to change.

To summarize, structuration theory gives us a conceptual lens through which we can understand how, and in what ways, the actions of individuals are related to the social structures in which those individuals are embedded (Giddens 1986). The process of structuration is a feedback process that may be accelerated or even constituted by viral events, which are the result of collective social sharing. When people behave according to norms in a particular social structure, say a community, it recursively reconstitutes that structure. When they do not, gaps occur in the structure, which feed back into the social structure and create opportunities for transformation.

Generally, social change is slow, and slippages in the social structure are exceedingly small. However, the speed, reach, and interconnectedness of social networks and the occurrence of viral events can accelerate the structuration processes. This doesn't imply that major social shifts will occur as a result of a single viral event, though we can't rule that out. What is more likely is that one viral event starts a *conversation* where people's *voice* is transmitted through the content they create and/or share. Perhaps a YouTube video or clever information visualization gives words to an existing underlying social discomfort. Once given voice, those who find that the content is salient to them, resonant with their views, or just *interesting*, share it with others and create an *interest network*. Some will create and share *response content*, most of which will receive little attention, but the few that manage to go viral will add to the evolving narrative of the network as people engage in collective sensemaking through the content they share. New shared content that manages to recontextualize the core ideas – memes – may further grow the interest network by making it salient, resonant or interesting to new clusters of people. Obscure individuals may find themselves in leadership roles as a result of the content they create; people separated by great distances may collaborate on the generation of new content; like-minded, geographically proximate individuals may choose to meet; collective action online may become collective action offline. In other words, behavior that would be marked "unconventional" for an isolated person may be normal when that person can connect to like-minded individuals in an interest network. This is one way that viral events may change social norms and social structures.

In this section we've given an overview of virality's role in the reproduction and transformation of social structure, but virality also impacts the structures of institutions, which is the topic for the next section.

Challenging institutions: Towards open government

Virality challenges and consequently fundamentally transforms structures of institutions. Before continuing, let's take one step back and differentiate between transformation of social structure and transformation of *institutions.* John Thompson, in his critique of Anthony Giddens' structuration theory, argued that "every act of production and reproduction may also be a potential act of transformation, as Giddens rightly insists; but the extent to which an action transforms an institution does *not* coincide with the extent to which social structure is thereby transformed" (Thompson 1984: 165). In other words, Thompson differentiates between the two aspects of social structures (as defined in the previous section): first, the norms, rules, practices, and arrangements through which the behavior of people is regulated in societies; and second, the structure of the institutions that are part of the fabric of society, the codes by which institutions operate. Institutions can be, for example, governments, media, public and private institutions (e.g., corporations), and even communities. This section focuses on the second element, the structure of institutions.

In the previous section we discussed how virality impacts social structure. Prevalent practices and values in society, as well as narratives of cultures and communities, are expressed by artifacts that go viral. Virality can be dual: it can reproduce while at the same time change norms and attitudes of people and their social structure.

When it comes to institutions, virality is less dual and

is mainly a driver of transformation. Virality at its core challenges the main structures of institutions embedded in our lives. Each one of these institutions is challenged in a distinct way by virality, which consequently drives them to be more accountable, transparent, and participatory. We illustrate this impact with two examples: the UC Davis pepper spray incident and the U.S. embassy cables leaked by WikiLeaks.

Viral events have the power to reach a large audience at a fast pace, much faster than traditional public institutions are used to. Moreover, for something to go viral it means that many people have viewed or engaged with it over a short period of time. So reach and speed together entail a strong power at the hands of individuals, not because of their separate ability to do things they previously couldn't, but because of the collective patterns of behavior that emerge from their individual actions (Nahon 2011). Individuals may not even be aware that they constitute a particular pattern. One person can take a photo, and another person can take a photo, but when hundreds of people take a photo of Lieutenant Pike pepper-spraying peaceful protesters from different angles, the outrage and reach and speed of the information brings the public to demand a fast response from the formal institutions and stakeholders involved. The day after the incident, the board of the UC Davis faculty issued a statement calling for two actions: one, "the immediate resignation of the Chancellor Katehi. The Chancellor's authorization of the use of police force to suppress the protests by students and community members speaking out on behalf of our university and public higher education generally represents

115

a gross failure of leadership"; two, "a policy that will end the practice of forcibly removing non-violent student, faculty, staff, and community protestors by police on the UC Davis campus" (DFA 2011). In September 2012, UC Davis reached a settlement with the protestors. In the settlement, the UC Davis Chancellor, Linda Katehi, issued a formal written apology to the protestors; the university agreed to pay $1 million as part of the settlement; and, most importantly, the university promised to work with the ACLU (American Civil Liberties Union) to develop new policies regarding student demonstrations, crowd management, and the use of force.

As for Lieutenant Pike, he was suspended with pay after the incident and on July 31, 2012, UC Davis' spokesperson announced that Pike was no longer employed by the university. The UC Davis police chief retired as well in April 2012, after a published report "found fault with much of the university leadership during the crisis" (Stanton 2012). So virality pushes for greater institutional accountability, and a checks-and-balances relationship between institutions (or their representatives) and the public. In recent years, the word "accountability" has become fashionable as a term that "expresses the continuing concern for checks and oversight, for surveillance and institutional constraints on the exercise of power" (Schedler and Plattner 1999: 13).[8] Accountability subjects *power* to the threat of sanctions, obliging it to be exercised in transparent ways, and forcing it to justify its acts. As a viral topic, the UC Davis pepper spray incident demonstrates this concept nicely. Not only because the event saw the light of the day, but because it demanded responses and justifications from both the university and the police, and sanctions were taken. Virality becomes a tool to conduct this process of citizen and individual monitoring of institutions. It forces institutions to be more accountable. When no standards of accountability are in place, the outrage of the public is what drives institutions to change and act (Castells 2012).

Since accountability's main dimension is *answerability*, it drives public officials to inform and to explain their actions. In democratic regimes, virality demands, almost forces, institutions to be more transparent and accountable. Governments have begun to internalize the public's expectation that they be more transparent. Of course governments are going to find ways to avoid being transparent (e.g., by introducing stricter controls, restricting access to smaller circles of individuals and groups). With regard to access and control of information, it is not a simple, one-way process: it's always been a struggle and it will, undoubtedly, continue to be. It's about power. States and governments exercise mechanisms of power, with respect to their citizens on a daily basis. However, social networking and the continuous threat of information being leaked and going viral increasingly challenge governments and, consequently, this changes the balance of power between states and citizens. The current and past structure of institutions is such that those institutions resist transparency but, as norms shift, there is increasing pressure on them to change. The request for transparency and accountability also happens in authoritarian regimes. Take, for example, the Arab Spring, which began in December 2010 and flooded most of the Arab countries. Rulers have been forced from power, and the structure of government has been transformed in Tunisia, Egypt, Libya, and Yemen; Syria is also possibly moving in this direction. For this discussion, however, we will focus only on democracies.

Like accountability, virality can increase the demand for more transparency from institutions. Transparency came to prominence after World War I in post-war negotiations (Braman 2009). While norms and values in recent years have been pushing towards transparency,[9] the change in institutional ecosystems is much slower (Bertot et al. 2012; Relly and Sabharwal 2009; Roberts 2006). It takes time for institutions to change and adapt to values like transparency and accountability. In the past two decades, an increasing number of governments have adopted "access-to-information laws at a pace unlike any other time in history" (Relly and Sabharwal 2009: 148). Governments may declare that they adopt principles of open government,[10] but the change in practices in this direction is much slower and faces many bureaucratic constraints in the attempt to transform rules and practices within institutions.

How can virality lead to more transparent institutional structures? Virality can reach millions of people quickly and make them pay attention and better understand information created by institutions. Transparency becomes the standard expectation of people as to how large institutions *should* behave. Government transparency generally occurs through one of the four primary channels: proactive dissemination by the government; release of requested materials by the government; public meetings; and leaks from whistleblowers (Piotrowski 2007). With easy-to-use devices that are able to capture information in various modes and ways, the threat of leaking becomes greater. For years, the dominant norm in big institutions, especially public institutions, was to control information (Barzilai-Nahon and Mason 2010). Open information was the exception. The memorandum about transparency and open government signed by U.S. President Barack Obama on May 2009 was a milestone (Obama 2009). It reflected a change in the way democratic political systems think: transparent public information is becoming the norm rather than the exception – even if only as declared, it still reflects a change. When coupled with easy-to-use visualizations, viral news stories can make difficult information clearer and easier to digest. The case of the WikiLeaks U.S. embassy cables can exemplify the struggle for power between public institutions and those requesting more transparency, and the response of the state to those demands. The threat of leaked information going viral acts as a mechanism that can change that balance of power. If and when institutions become more transparent, leaked information and virality become less of a threat, and then less effective at transforming institutions.

On November 28, 2010, WikiLeaks[11] and five prominent newspapers (*The New York Times*, *The Guardian*, *Der Speigel*, *Le Monde*, and *El País*) simultaneously began to publish hundreds of dispatches from more than 250 U.S. embassies and consulates, sent since 1960. The dataset today includes 251,287 dispatches. The diplomatic cables revealed juicy secrets, such as how the U.S.

refers to other states and leaders in the world, and more generally addressed issues of external political relations, internal government affairs, economic conditions, terrorists and terrorism, foreign trade, and intelligence.[12] Needless to say, some of the leaked cables caused tremendous embarrassment to the U.S. For example, Vladimir Putin, Russia's President, was described as an "alpha dog"; Angela Merkel, Chancellor of Germany, was referred to as "Teflon Merkel"; and Nicolas Sarkozy, France's former President, was called an "emperor."

During the last week of November 2010, something interesting happened. Governments worldwide were waiting impatiently for the publication of the 250,000 classified and unclassified cables in social networks.[13] The avalanche of leaked information began with *The Guardian*, which allowed users without high-level digital skills to dissect the data. *The Guardian* customized an application of maps (by using Google Fusion tables), which enabled the investigation and analysis of the classified cables by date and country.[14] This helped tremendously in making this information viral. It also allowed users to download either all of the original information or the information with metadata (tags that help one more easily understand the data) that the newspaper itself added.

With such large and comprehensive amounts of data, journalists understood that it was no longer enough to summarize main events to readers, as they used to do in the past.[15] Actually, it was not possible to summarize that much data, even if they wanted to. Instead, they made the data accessible and transformed readers from *passive* to *active* users, who could dissect data and share the information they found relevant with others. This crowdsourcing is exactly the process that transforms information from anonymous to viral and known to many. Manuel Castells, a prominent network society researcher, noted in an interview that "what is wiki is the leaks, not the publication itself." This reflects well the participatory nature of topics that become viral; not only in sharing but in participating in making the information accessible to other people around the world. It gives users the impression that they are participating in the act of change.

In our example, WikiLeaks has challenged the state's control of information. As an aftereffect, the U.S. government changed its security regulations among agencies to address gaps in the policies of information systems security, including the detection of internal threats to information security. It has also issued new regulations regarding communication methods among embassies and other agencies that handle classified information.[16] "The government's position was (and remains) that the classified portions of the disclosures remain classified until properly declassified, even though the information was now widely in the public domain. The office of Management and Budget (OMB) issued stern warnings to federal employees to not view, and especially to not download, the documents on non-secure computers" (McDermott et al. 2011: 9).

The WikiLeaks incident has powerful implications for the relationship between states and citizens, as well as the relationships between states. The new continuous deterrence of uncovering internal communications and going viral in public can cause bureaucrats to be more careful in the way they express themselves both internally and externally, and may drive public institutions to activate new methods of information control to keep it away from the public's eyes, like in the WikiLeaks case. But at the same time, the structure of the institutions do change. They begin to internalize the public's expectation for transparency and the accountability of the expressions and actions of their officials. In some cases, the challenge may create an opposite effect by institutionalizing greater practices of transparency, accountability, and participation, like in the UC Davis pepper spray incident.

While institutions are challenged by virality in ways that drives them to be more accountable, transparent, and participatory, virality also pushes institutions to become more social. By *social* we mean that public (e.g., governments) and private (e.g., corporations) institutions need to find ways to engage with their citizens and consumers. Hemsley and Mason (2012) use virality as a conceptual tool to argue that organizations that assume that social media represents another one-way communication channel, like TV or radio, risk falling behind. Being social is listening, attending to the concerns of the community, and taking ownership and responsibility where appropriate. As we saw from the "United Breaks Guitars" example, organizations that fail to *listen* and respond to the concerns of their clients risk the cumulative hours of bad publicity that a single viral event can cause.

Viral events can bring both positive and negative attention to people, their families, corporations, and other organizations. Attention, though, is a fickle thing. Virality has a life cycle. All viral events naturally decay as the attention that fuels them wanes. But, as we shall see in the final chapter, viral events don't truly die.

7

Afterlife

Up to this point in the book, we have focused mainly on that brief period of time in the life cycle of virality that gets the most attention: the peak and the lead up to the peak. This period is exciting as connections are constructed and information starts to diffuse. However, this growth in attention cannot last forever. At some point, a decay phase begins. The decay rate varies from one viral event to another, but is typically more gradual than the ramp-up phase (for further discussion of this, see chapter 2). The journey of information from obscurity to fame ends with loss of public interest. However, this is only the end of the first chapter in the life cycle of virality, and the rest of the phases (i.e., the decay, afterlife, and revival phases) are just as important to consider. These phases have implications for our lives and can illuminate aspects of our behavior as individuals and collectives. What happens when viral information falls into the abyss of oblivion? Why do viral events decay at all? Where does the past-viral content reside and what does this mean for us as individuals and for researchers?

And most importantly, to what extent can virality serve societies as an institutionalizing mechanism of public and individual memories?

In this last chapter of the book, we will explore the phases after the peak, beginning with the decay phase, and then examine the (for want of a better phrase) *afterlife* and revival phases of viral events. We will finish the book by offering a theoretical framework useful for thinking about and explaining virality, which also summarizes the main threads of this book. We hope that the theoretical framework will ignite future dialogue about virality and its impact.

Inevitable decay

Readers may find our choice of the word "decay" an odd one. Even after the peak of a viral event, people continue to consume the content and the number of cumulative views continues to rise. However, what is *decaying* is the *rate of growth* of the number of views that a viral event receives. At present, there are few studies that examine the decay phase (Crane and Sornette 2008; Deschâtres and Sornette 2005) and none, that we know of, explicitly compares what happens in the growth phase to what happens in the decay phase. This should definitely become an area for future work, since the pace and shape of the decay phase hold important clues about the viral process and its impact. As an example, different categories of content (e.g., how-to videos and music videos) tend to have longer sharing chains, which may result in shorter peaks but a longer decay phase.

Decay is inevitable, but why? There are practical limits on the magnitude of a viral event that originate in human behavior. Some of these limits are the subject of more than 60 years of research in behavioral organization theory, behavioral decision theory, survey research, and experimental economics. As far back as 1955, the scientist Herbert Simon proposed that decision-making behavior should be viewed as bounded rational. Simon argued that the rationality of individuals is limited by the lack of full information, the lack of time to make a rational decision, and the limited capabilities and skills to analyze information. Over the years the topic has become a well-explored area of research, and has expanded into the study of the cognitive and social biases of behavior of people; these systematic biases separate people's actual beliefs and choices from those desired (Jones 1999; Kahneman 2003). Some of these behavioral limitations are related directly to the decay of viral information. Let's explore this further.

Following in the footsteps of Herbert Simon, the psychologist Warren Thorngate argued that with so much content available, on so many different media channels and platforms, the amount of information available to people is far greater than people's ability to attend to it (Thorngate 1988). Thorngate developed principles of *attentional economics*, three of which are relevant to our discussion. The first, the idea of *diminishing attention returns*, implies that the value gained from paying attention to an information item diminishes the longer we pay attention to it. As new information items arise, our attention shifts from old items, whose value has diminished, to new items, with the result that those older items tend to fall out of the public's awareness. It is true that we watch some videos more than once, but by and large, once we have seen something, we don't tend to watch it again. Viral events decay because of people's diminishing attention to the content, though likely not to the same extent as non-viral events.

The next principle, the principle of *fixed attentional assets*, extends itself as well from the bounded rationality school of thought and states that "attention is a finite and a non-renewable resource" (Thorngate 1988: 248). This means that our capability to pay attention to everything is limited, so eventually we must stop paying attention to some things in order to pay attention to others. This is particularly true these days, as content is created and shared constantly, every second of the day. We can also think of this in terms of competitive crowding out, another concept from economics (Birchler and Bütler 2007). Here the idea is simply that new content is always competing with older content for our attention, so new content, which we perceive as more valuable (see the first principle above) crowds out the old content.

Finally, Thorngate's principle of *singular attentional investments* states that people will generally pay attention to one item at a time. As an example, how many videos on YouTube can you watch simultaneously? Are you suspicious when you look over and your teenager says they are doing homework while tapping out a message on their smartphone with a video playing on the laptop? The mainstream research on the topic still suggests that humans are not capable of *true* multitasking (Medina 2009). Instead, we pay attention to one thing at a time, paying a switching cost each time we move our attention from one thing to another. If we could truly multitask, we could watch a TED video, reread last week's edition of *The Economist*, and listen to a podcast of BBC's World News all at the same time. Being able to cognitively digest multiple channels of media simultaneously would reduce the crowding out effect mentioned above. There would be less competitive pressure on older content such that we would expect that the decay phase would be lengthened. The characteristics of virality (being remarkable, socially shared, and discussed), indicate that these attentional biases are weaker for viral content compared to non-viral content. Yet, these attentional limitations would be one of the main causes of information decay.

Attentional limitations are important in explaining why viral content decays, but other explanations ought to be considered as well. The first of these explanations is culture (in the large sense of it). By now we have enough studies that provide evidence of cross-cultural differences in using social networks and watching content (Qiu et al. 2013; Segev et al. 2007; Vasalou et al. 2010). Cultural walls that some content cannot pass through likely bound the magnitude of viral events, as well. In chapter 6, we mentioned the viral Korean *Gangnam Style* video clip. The video received unbelievable attention (roughly 1.4 billion views). However, the subtlety of the narratives told in that video are largely invisible to non-Korean audiences. Additionally, according to the video statistics on YouTube, female and male teenagers are the main group watching the video. The same goes with the video of KONY2012, which we will discuss later in this chapter. The video was top-watched by people from the United States, United Kingdom, and Canada. Indeed, most content, whether viral or not, is bounded by the language, norms and values, and the shared history that represent collectives. What is remarkable or funny to an individual from one culture may be considered repellant to someone from another culture. When it comes to viral content, these differences serve also as the boundaries to the ability of the content to continue its inertia of growing attention. After exhausting possible audiences for viral content, the decay begins.

Afterlife: Institutionalizing public and individual memory

What happens after the decay phase? In general, the content still exists on the Internet as a kind of monument to a very specific nexus in time and context in which enough people thought that it was so remarkable they shared it among their social networks. It also resides in the memories of the individuals and crowds that participated in the collective action, which created the viral event. Even when the vast majority of people have forgotten about it, viral content often continues to receive a small amount of attention. The afterlife period is a semi-dormant period of time; however, virality can be revived and return to the center of attention at any given moment.

The afterlife of viral content is very different from that of other types of content. Why? When viral information decays, it preserves a high degree of stickiness in the web ecology, much higher than non-viral information; sticky, as it is practically impossible to delete it from the network sphere, where it resides in different modes, forms, technologies, and places. There are two main reasons for the extra-sticky characteristic of viral information. First, as discussed earlier, viral information is socially resistant to control. Once the information becomes viral, we lose the ability to control the path of its expansion as it travels through many networks and many hands. It becomes a topic for conversations, discussions, and rumors. People talk about it, mention it, share it, and write posts about it. Each and every such action is another instantiation of the ecology of the viral item and more firmly fixes and preserves it on our networks' "walls of fame." Each time people create another recording, archive, or copy, they facilitate the process of uncovering it later. Second, virality is evidence that the content was perceived as interesting enough for certain crowds of people to pay attention. As such, it may become a signal as to what is important to parts of societies at certain points in time. As the viral content is perceived as an important artifact, it is handled with additional care. Institutions archive it while adding identifying tags; organizations publish statistics about it; scientists analyze it; and people copy and save it on their personal hard disks. These additional actions strengthen the stickiness of the item. The careful digital curation, the special preservation and maintenance of past-viral artifacts, makes it easier to find years after.

Viktor Mayer-Schönberger argues that, "since the beginning of time, for us humans, forgetting has been the norm and remembering the exception. Because of digital technology and global networks, however, this balance has shifted. Today with the help of widespread technology, forgetting has become the exception, and remembering the default" (2009: 2). The loss of public attention does not lead necessarily to forgetting, as the content and experience may well stay in our memory, and is ready to be easily retrieved. At the same time, stickiness, the impossibility of deletion, does not assure remembrance by individuals and collectives. The direct link between the stickiness of viral information and remembrance, or the return to the public conscious-ness, is not straightforward. Easy-to-use technologies facilitate the process of replicating, making viral infor-mation scalable and more searchable than non-viral information. Consequently, these three affordances also facilitate the return to the public eye, as they make the process of retrieving viral information from the web, once it has died out, simple, and allow the content to re-gain attention. If searchability did not exist, then once an item (e.g., a photo) lost its novelty or newsworthi-ness, it could fall out of the public's awareness and, even with persistence as a feature of the networked public, a viral photo would become obscure and forgotten. These three affordances allow that photo to return to the public awareness over and over. The information is there, and now all that is needed is a contextual stimulus to motivate people to rediscover this information, which may start a new cycle of sharing and distributing.

One of the remaining mysteries to be investigated is: What are we left with after viral information decays? What do we remember? Science has not yet addressed these questions rigorously, and so our discussion draws mainly from the evidence of our cases. Let's examine these questions through the case of the viral video of KONY2012.

KONY2012 is a 30-minute documentary viral video, which reached over 100 million views, from around 750 copies scattered across the web, in six days. The video was produced by a nonprofit advocacy group, Invisible Children, founded in 2004 with the aim of increasing awareness of, and putting an end to, the practices of the Lord's Resistance Army (LRA) in Central Africa and arresting its leader Joseph Kony. The International Criminal Court (ICC) issued warrants for the arrest of Joseph Kony and other leaders in the group as far back as 2005, but even as we write, Joseph Kony has not been brought to justice. The LRA group was accused of human rights violations and, according to the ICC, it "has established a pattern of brutalization of civilians by acts including murder, abduction, sexual enslavement, mutilation, as well as mass burnings of houses and looting of camp settlements; that abducted civilians, including children, are said to have been forcibly recruited as fighters, porters and sex slaves and to take part in attacks against the Ugandan army (UPDF) and civilian communities" (International Criminal Court 2005).

The KONY2012 video is part of a larger campaign to increase public awareness about Joseph Kony and bring him to justice by the end of 2012. The video was professionally edited and carries a compelling message[1] with the following narrative – we live in an information era in which "we share what we love and it reminds us what we have in common." In order to bring Kony in for arrest, the video informs viewers that enough people need to know about him and his crimes. The filmmaker and narrator of KONY2012, Jason Russell, declares that "99% of the planet doesn't know who Kony is. If they did, he would have been stopped years ago." In other words, Jason Russell argued that if a critical mass of people became aware of the story, it would create pressure on the U.S. government to help the Uganda military find and arrest Kony. The video ends with a message to the audience – *each one of you can make a difference by simply sharing the video.*

The video is compelling and went viral because "it offers an extremely simple narrative: Kony is a uniquely bad actor, a horrific human being, whose capture will end suffering for the people of Northern Uganda. If each of us does our part, influences powerful people, the world's most powerful military force will take action and Kony will be captured" (Zuckerman 2012).

An interesting question is: What is left in the minds of the people who watched and shared the KONY2012 video? More generally, what do we remember from viral content?

Humans tend to remember moments that made a difference for them more than routinized moments (Kahneman 2010; Miron-Shatz et al. 2009). For example, if the movie created negative or positive emotions, it would probably increase the chances of people remembering it later. When we remember a movie, there is a gap between what we remember about the movie and what we felt at the time we watched the movie. Kahneman and colleagues refer to this as the memory-experience gap (Kahneman et al. 1993; Redelmeier and Kahneman 1996; Redelmeier et al. 2003). "The experiencing-self lives continuously, having one experience after the other, while the remembering-self is an evaluator, keeps scores of our experiences, and crafts stories from the moments that made a difference to us" (Kahneman 2010). While we can go back and watch the KONY2012 movie again and affirm or refute what our memory tells us about it, it is likely that we won't do it unless we have a good reason. So, our memory of the KONY2012 video will comprise certain special moments, the ones that are significant for us.

But KONY2012 is not just another movie. It is a viral movie. A viral event is also remembered inter alia *because it went viral*, not just because of its content. The fact that it was viral by itself changes the experience. In other words, when we watched KONY2012, part of the experience was the fact that many other millions had also watched it, as if being part of a crowd gives the content an imagined credibility in terms of its interest and importance. Thus, our memory remembers not only the significant parts of the content, but also its status as a viral event. These two different experiences, experiencing the virality of the video and experiencing the content, blend into one individual memory. Needless to say, this increases our chances of remembering the movie in the first place. Additionally, at its core, a viral event is a social experience. As such, communities of interest (i.e., communities associated with us, people) interpret the message of the viral event during its life cycle. Our experience of it as individuals is impacted by the collective experience of our community. So too is our memory of it, which may include not only our individual memories of the viral event but also our collective ones as well. Once the viral event decays, what is left includes the many copies and derivatives of the information, commentaries made about it, and communal and institutional interpretations, which are archived and categorized for future public access.

Therefore, virality as a process can be regarded as another mechanism (among others) of institutionalizing individual and collective memories. "Combine accessibility and durability, and humans can no longer successfully run away from their past" (Mayer-Schönberger 2009: 103). In fact, if we assume that virality can signal what is considered important and interesting to parts of a society[2] at a particular time, then traces of viral content may also become a way of documenting the fabric of societies. Let's explore this in more detail. *Actions* by users related to the viral event – links, comments, interpretations, user self-generated tags, memes, and conversations – are all reflections of the process of sensemaking of the individuals involved in the viral event. Observing these actions can help us understand the sensemaking process that people employed to the environments they were embedded in. For example, linking to a viral video and adding a comment can tell us about how a particular person feels, how they framed and interpreted the meaning of the viral event. Comments on Twitter like "Just watched the KONY2012 video. In tears and I want to help make a difference. Make KONY famous" or "we have to make kony famous, so the police can arrest him. #stopkony" can tell us that these people were touched by the video and that they believed that action against Kony should be taken. These tweets are observable traces of the sensemaking process that these people have gone through while watching the viral video.

We can think of each of these comments, links, etc., as an instantiation of the sensemaking process related to the KONY video. In doing so, we could cluster individual narratives into groups: people who thought Kony is a person that should be stopped, people who felt sorry for the kids, people who didn't believe the filmmakers, etc. These could then be mapped into *collective sensemaking clusters*, each of which represents the *meaning* that crowds construct for a particular event. The sensemaking actions of crowds, as well as the careful preservation of the viral content, effectively documents the fabric of societies; what crowds think, feel, and interpret; or what streams (groups that evolve over time) exist in societies. Therefore, over a matter of years, the preservation of viral events and their ecosystems could become not only the mechanism for institutionalizing collective memory, but also a mechanism that facilitates an understanding of the fabric of societies, the narratives of crowds, and how those two are related.

When we retrieve these events from the network's memory in the future, we will see the many voices and narratives that interpreted and categorized the event, with their social and political biases embedded in it. Certainly the politics of current-day categorization will play a role in how the future makes sense of what they find. These events not only comprise social and political biases, but will also contain representations of the event that could include disinformation (deceptive information) and misinformation (inaccurate or incomplete information). Soon after its release, the KONY2012 video became controversial and was criticized for being inaccurate, oversimplified, and refocusing charity work in less effective ways. Ethan Zuckerman wrote in his blog: "It is a story about simplification and framing" (Zuckerman 2012). For example, Joseph Kony had not been in Uganda since 2006, and the LRA group numbered at most in the hundreds (Wilkerson 2012; Zuckerman 2012). Invisible Children was also questioned for its motives, transparency, and spending of funds. Now ask yourself, how many of the people who saw KONY2012 are aware of the disinformation and misinformation in the movie? Thus, disinformation and misinformation inform and crystallize our opinions during the sensemaking process. The representation of the fabric of societies has errors, biases, and contradictions embedded within.

Finally, viral events may have more than *one soul*. While this is rare, content can go viral multiple times (see figure 7.1). For example, the video "Yes We Can Obama Song", by the singer Will.I.Am, was released in February 2008 and became one of the most viral videos during the 2008 U.S. Presidential election cycle. The lyrics in the video are quotations from Barack Obama's concession speech in the New Hampshire Presidential primary. The video has gone viral three times so far: the first peak happened within a few days of its release; it peaked a second time on Election Day; and the third, a semi-viral spike, happened almost three months later, on January 21, the day of the inauguration ceremony of Barack Obama as the 44th President of the United States. In between the peaks, the video was not totally

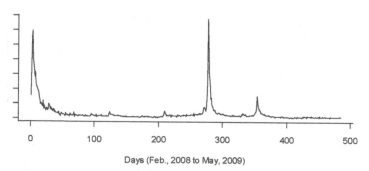

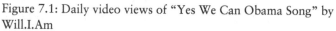

Days (Feb., 2008 to May, 2009)

Figure 7.1: Daily video views of "Yes We Can Obama Song" by Will.I.Am

forgotten. A relatively small number of views trickled in daily. The re-acceleration to another viral cycle was contingent upon political events. Once again, context and timing were key, and once an event goes viral again, the cycle ends, and returns to the beginning.

Going viral: The bigger picture

In this book, we have attempted to convey the complex facets of virality in an accessible language for social scientists and the general public. We have drawn on the work of a great number of researchers to support our main arguments. Figure 7.2 encapsulates the main elements of virality discussed throughout the book. While trying to summarize the complexities of virality with a single illustration may endanger our project through over-simplification, it also offers some benefits. The most important of these is having a theoretical framework that can stimulate discussion and serve as a foundation for future research on virality.

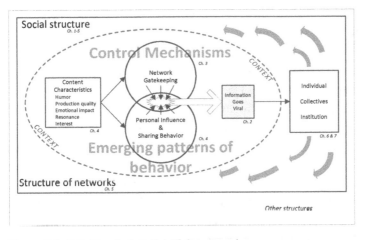

Figure 7.2: Virality: A theoretical framework

Virality is a consequence of dialogue and tension between many forces. The main tension occurs between the emergent sharing patterns of users (usually constituted through bottom-up processes) and the control mechanisms exerted on information flows (usually driven by top-down processes, e.g. network gatekeeping and social and network structures). Most of the evidence we present in this book shows that network gatekeeping is crucial to the formation of nearly all viral events. Network gatekeeping connects networks and can therefore broaden the range of users and the number of networks exposed to the information. Network gatekeeping is also about selecting and choosing content to present, and even promote, which can serve as an enabler in the viral process. While gatekeepers are a crucial component of information diffusion, once social sharing reaches a critical mass and the viral process starts, viral content is socially resistant to the control of information flows and can circumvent gatekeepers (see chapter 3 for more discussion about network gatekeeping). But this is only part of the story.

The other part consists of emerging patterns of human behavior. The *bottom-up perspective* focuses on the patterns of sharing behavior within crowds that also drive viral events. While gatekeepers are needed to make people aware of content, social interactions between people are a fundamental aspect of viral events – without social sharing, virality does not happen. Stated differently, you can still have information diffusion without social sharing, it just isn't viral information diffusion. These patterns of sharing behavior, once constituted, become control mechanisms by themselves because they ultimately alter the social structures in which we all live.

An on-going dialogue and tension exists between these forces. Sometimes gatekeepers attempt to promote content that doesn't engage people; often people make content that never spreads beyond their circle of friends. Viral events need some mix of both. But this doesn't mean that there is a 50-50 mix of top-down, bottom-up factors for each event. Instead, each viral event will be a product of a unique mix that depends on the nature of the content, who opts to share the message and their position in social networks, as well as the timing of the message and the surrounding *context*. Context is the unique circumstances that form the setting of a particular event (e.g., physical, social, cultural, psychological, or related history) and can make or break a viral event. The likelihood of going viral increases as these forces align; when both the crowd and the gatekeepers indicate something is important by sharing it, and context enables it, truly large-scale viral events can occur: think Susan Boyle's audition and PSY's *Gangnam Style* video.

At its core, virality relies on social interactions. As such, it operates within the framework of the structure of networks and the structure of society. Shared values, norms, and other social agreements may serve as the engine of virality, but at the same time they bound information flows, which effectively controls and limits viral events according to their own codex. If we think back over some of the viral examples in this book, the most remarkable ones reached tens of millions of people in an incredibly short time frame (e.g., Susan Boyle and *Gangnam Style*). It is easy to dismiss most viral events as entertainment, but in chapter 4 we demonstrated that even entertainment can reflect important cultural values, and in chapter 6 we showed that entertainment reproduces social norms.

Virality, then, is a mechanism that reproduces social norms, but it can also be a mechanism that challenges institutions and their structure. One outcome of a viral event is an interest network, which through repeated viral events or simply as a result of the discussions that accompany viral events, can form more durable networks that support sharing, collaboration, and, in some cases, even collective action. These kinds of durable interest networks may be a factor in the pressure that was successfully applied at UC Davis. They may also have been part of what supported the growth of recent movements like Occupy Wall Street. Many people see this kind of emergent collective action as a positive outcome assisted by the ability to quickly share information, with many people, on a distributed network. In other words, viral events may play a role in events that destabilize traditional institutions not only by spreading information, but also by bringing people together who share common concerns or grievances. Since virality spreads quickly and is resistant to control, it may have the power to circumvent the regulatory power of the prevailing social structure. As the UC Davis pepper spray incident highlighted, when enough people suddenly become aware of abuses of power, they can band together and quickly produce enough pressure to fundamentally alter the structures of organizations and institutions.

At the very start of this book, we said that virality isn't new. We suggested that examples of information that spread quickly and reached many people through social sharing could be found in instances such as the spread of the news of Rosa Parks' arrest in 1955. So virality is not new. What is new is that information technologies, when seen collectively, have formed a social infrastructure that facilitates the sharing, speed, and reach that are fundamental to viral events. By their very nature, viral events reflect what people think is worth paying attention to, what is right and what is wrong with the world. Virality is part of our everyday social landscape and it is here to stay.

Notes

Chapter 1 Introduction: Virality of pets and presidents

1 http://www.youtube.com/watch?v=RxPZh4AnWyk
2 http://homerecording.about.com/od/tricksofthepros/a/
  Was-Susan-Boyle-Auto-Tuned-on-Britains-Got-Talent.
  htm
3 http://www.huffingtonpost.com/letty-cottin-pogrebin/
  why-susan-boyle-makes-us_b_187790.html
4 Posted Sunday March 13, 2001, http://www.youtube.
  com/watch?v=zQR01qltgo8
5 http://www.huffingtonpost.com/2011/03/14/alexandra-
  wallace-racist-video_n_835505.html
6 @ReallyVirtual (2011, May 1, 00:58 PKT). Helicopter
  hovering above Abbottabad at 1AM (is a rare event).
  [Twitter post]. Retrieved from https://twitter.com/
  ReallyVirtual/status/64780730286358528 on October 7,
  2012.
7 http://abcnews.go.com/Politics/target-bin-laden-death-
  life-osama-bin-laden/story?id=13786598&singlePage=t
  rue#.UG_VLflrZhw
8 @keithurbahn (2011, May 1, 22:24 EDT). "So I'm told

by a reputable person they have killed Osama Bin Laden. Hot Damn." [Twitter post]. Retrieved from https://twitter.com/keithurbahn/status/64877790624886784 on October 6, 2012.

9 @brianStelter (2011, May 1). Chief of staff for former defense sec. Rumsfeld, @keithurbahn, tweets: "I'm told by a reputable person they have killed Osama Bin Laden" [Twitter post]. Retrieved from https://twitter.com/brian stelter/status/64878223787425792 on October 6, 2012.

10 http://www.youtube.com/watch?v=5YGc4zOqozo

11 http://www.blogan.net/blog/2009/07/taylor-guitars-responds-to-united-breaks-guitars/

12 http://www.lipsticking.com/2009/07/united-breaks-gui tars-a-great-video-from-the-sons-of-maxwell-group.html

13 http://www.neatorama.com/2009/07/08/united-breaks-guitars/

14 This is a version of an analysis that first appeared on http://www.stevewoda.com/2009/07/poor-customer-service-goes-viral.html

Chapter 2: What Virality Is: I know it when I see it

1 http://www.youtube.com/watch?v=a_uzUh1VT98

2 http://www.youtube.com/watch?v=9Ek61w1LxSc

3 By *sharp acceleration* we mean that the rate at which a viral item is viewed in a specific time period is significantly larger than the previous time period. As an example, if we plot the number of views per day for a viral video, the slop of the plotted line would quickly turn sharply up (for example, see figure 2.4). Mathematically it is possible to identify viral content candidates by fitting the view data from the peak forward to a power-law, and then estimating the *shape parameter*. A simple power-law

is given by 1/xα, where α is the shape parameter. Alpha values from 0.2 to 0.6 indicate a critical mass in sharing has been reached. Why?

Crane and Sornette (2008) studied views-over-time for more than 5 million videos on YouTube and were able to categorize videos into a two-by-two matrix based on whether the distribution of views-per-day (or signature) represented an endogenous or exogenous event on the first dimension, with the second dimension indicating whether or not the video reached a critical mass of sharing. They assume that people arrive at YouTube videos according to one of three cases: random way, endogenously (through social sharing) or exogenously (the video is featured or otherwise promoted). They also assume that viral videos are those that fit into the endogenous-critical category (with a shape parameter of 0.2) and refer to videos in the exogenous-critical category as "quality" videos ($\alpha = 0.6$). In other words, according to their view only videos that reach a critical mass without being featured (or otherwise promoted) can be considered viral. However, as we will argue in the coming chapters, this is an overly simplistic view. As the Susan Boyle video demonstrates, content that is promoted in the mainstream media can still go viral as people share and reshare it into their social networks. It should be noted that the exogenous-critical category includes videos with a shape parameters clustered around 0.6, and that the endogenous-critical category includes videos with a shape parameters clustered around 0.2. Thus, if a video's α was 0.19, we may still consider it a candidate for inclusion into a set of viral events. See Clauset et al. (2009) for techniques for estimating α using maximum likelihood estimators (MLE) techniques.

4 This definition draws on work done by Hemsley and Mason (2012) and Nahon et al. (2011). It synthesizes

common themes that arise in marketing and network science literature as well more recent quantitative work that has explored information flows more generally on specific platforms like Twitter (Asur et al. 2011; Bakshy et al. 2011; Kwak et al. 2010), Facebook (Bakshy et al. 2012), email (Huberman and Adamic 2004), blogs (Leskovec et al. 2007b), and YouTube (Broxton et al. 2010; Crane and Sornette 2008).

5 While Jurvetson and Draper (1997) are often credited with popularizing the term viral, other marketers used the term as much as decade earlier. See Kirby and Marsden (2012) for more details.

6 We note that not every *follower* is actually *exposed* for a variety of reasons that we discuss later.

7 Crane and Sornette (2008) are actually looking at endogenous and exogenous signatures, but they equate endogenous with word of mouth, or sharing within social networks. Broxton et al. (2010) do use the phrase *social* and *socialness* in their look at ratios of different types of referral data. Their work shows similar signatures for social vs. non-social sharing.

8 Another example of this sharp take-off in a set of promoted videos can be found in Boynton (2009).

9 The mathematical way to express this is $f(x) = ax$, where a is the number of people on each round sharing, and x is the round. So for a game with broad enough appeal, where each person sharing it, ten new people share it as well, we would have $10^5 = 100,000$ in just five rounds.

10 Formally, a power-law is a probability distribution in the form of $f(x) = 1/xk$, where k is called the shape parameter. Visually (see figure 2.5 and 5.3), a power-law is characterized in a graph by a tall peak on the left that slopes sharply downward and then levels off as the line of the graph goes to the right. As an example, a social scientist

would use a power-law to represents the idea that a few people attract the majority of attention.

11 See previous note about what is meant by *sharp accelera-tion*.

12 In figure 2.3 we plotted the daily views for the video for the first month, as well as a moving average to show that the growth and decline in daily views is more closely related to the social profile than the promoted profile. The dip in views around Saturday, May 29 and Sunday, May 30, 2010, reflects the fact that people don't spend as much time online during the weekends.

13 This represents an interesting kind of emerging advertis-ing where for just a few dollars anyone can promote a message in a targeted way, or, as we have seen before, for large amounts of money big companies can find ways to insert their ad messages into people's social feeds.

14 See Watts (2004) for a detailed description of the role of "percolating clusters" in diffusion.

15 See chapter 11 of *Connected Marketing* (Kirby and Marsden 2012) for a detailed examination of the his-torical use of the term word-of-mouth as well as a careful examination of the generally accepted definition.

16 For some examples, see http://www.buzzfeed.com/mjs 538/the-pepper-spraying-cop-meme, http://www.tumblr. com/tagged/pepper%20spray%20cop, http://www.tum blr.com/tagged/occupy%20uc%20davis and http://www. flickr.com/search/?q=Lt.%20Pike.

Chapter 3: What Makes Something Viral I: The control of networks through gatekeeping

1 In figure 3.3, the solid line at the top shows the total number of times Keith Urbahn's tweet was retweeted,

per minute for 30 minutes. The heavy dashed line shows the number of times people directly retweeted Keith's tweet (1,205). The dotted line shows the number of direct retweets of Brian Stelter's tweet – a retweet itself (1,010). The remaining volume (thin dash-dot-dot line) are retweets of the retweets and make up a bit more than half of the total tweets over this 30-minute period.

2 SocialFlow's analysis suggests that as many as 15 million tweets had been sent between the time of Dan Pfeiffer's tweet and when the President addressed the nation.

3 In the figure 3.3 we note that Keith Urbahn's tweet received 1,852 direct retweets, but at the time he only had 1,016 followers. We account for this by noting that when people retweet a message using Twitter's retweet button, the message is attributed to the person who posted the original tweet. As an example, if Karine retweets a message from her friend Limor, and Jeff reads Karine's tweet and retweets it, both Karine and Jeff's tweets will indicate that they came from Limor. In the case of Keith Urbahn, it won't matter how many clusters Urbahn's tweet hopped, Twitter will always report that users retweeted Keith.

4 http://www.flickr.com/photos/twitteroffice/5681263084/

5 http://www.guardian.co.uk/technology/2011/may/09/lessons-from-bin-laden-coverage

6 For a careful analysis supporting this, see Wu et al. (2012).

Chapter 4: What Makes Something Viral II: What is everyone looking at?

1 http://www.youtube.com/watch?v=5YGc4zOqozo

2 http://blogan.net/blog/2009/07/taylor-guitars-responds-to-united-breaks-guitars/

3 http://www.lipsticking.com/2009/07/united-breaks-gui
   tars-a-great-video-from-the-sons-of-maxwell-group.html
4 For example, see "London Riots – Manchester Riot
   Police Beat Teenagers On Bikes," http://www.youtube.
   com/watch?v=QgXpNqT2kJE. Also, note that a search
   on YouTube for "London Riots" returned over 50,000
   videos.
5 As an example, see "Sliding Cars in Seattle Snow on
   11/22/10", http://www.youtube.com/watch?v=rhZCyQ3
   emQg. Watch for the bus at 2:48.
6 http://www.r-project.org/
7 http://www.youtube.com/watch?v=XX9hc5lkNSo
8 http://www.r-bloggers.com/
9 YouTube offers no insight into what a referral from
   Google means. It could be from Google Plus, but these
   numbers also reflect cases where someone saw the video
   and wanted to see it again or show it to someone else
   but didn't have the URL at hand. If people search for the
   video and then show it to someone else, this is also a kind
   of social sharing.
10 YouTube sources include referrals for similar videos as
   well as all the times we interacted with the video ourselves.
11 In many cases the literature of marketing uses the word
   influence, but from our perspective their view of it is too
   narrow and often is focused only on getting people to
   behave in a specific way, for example, to buy a product,
   to share content, to recommend a product, click on a like,
   etc. However, the concept of influence is much larger
   and complex. Lukes suggests that "influence exists where
   A, without resorting to either a tacit or overt threat of
   severe deprivation, causes B to change his course of
   action" (Lukes 2005: 22), and Katz suggests that there
   are multiple forms of influence, of which he focuses on

imitation, contagion, persuasion, and manipulation (Katz and Lazarsfeld 1955: xxi). Thus, influencing the behavior or norms of people can happen with or without resistance, as a consequence of actions, and, finally, inactions can also shape and influence one's preferences and awareness, and thus their behavior. For a thorough review on different facets of power, see Lukes (2005).

12 In chapter 3, we discussed network gatekeepers, and their role in the viral process. We argued that "one common element is that certain actors can exercise greater control over the flow of information than others, and as such, they have a disproportionate amount of influence." Within the context of gatekeepers, influence occurs as a direct result of the information control practices. But influence is a word with many meanings (see previous note), and can occur under a variety of situations and conditions, for example, because we trust or admire someone. In this chapter, we use the word "influence" in a general way and as occurring between people. Within our conceptual breakdown, this is a bottom-up perspective and usually happens in a non-purposeful manner. We note that the dichotomy of top-down/bottom-up is artificial and, thus, if any boundary exists between them, it is a fuzzy one. For conceptual purposes, we suggest that intentional acts aimed at altering another person's behavior fits better in the top-down perspective, but again, this is not absolute.

13 Note that while Christakis and Fowler's work is interesting, the question of whether or not we can actually use statistical methods to distinguish between homophily and influence (or social contagion/imitation) has been called into question. For more information, see Shalizi and Thomas (2011) and Aral et al. (2009).

Chapter 5: What Makes Something Viral III: Caught in the viral net!

1 We use the word regulated in a multifaceted way. First, we refer to self-regulation as an internal control mechanism that governs what behavior is performed. Self-regulation occurs through the interplay of self-produced and external sources of influence, including motivational standards and social and moral standards (Bandura 1989). This also captures the idea that rules, practices, and arrangements can be directive, enabling some behaviors while discouraging or ruling out others.

2 For more information, see Nahon et al. (2011), but also note that the blog scale we started with was derived from Karpf (2008).

3 Link distributions in social networks vary depending on many factors. For example, Kwak et al. (2010) found that a follower network on Twitter did not fit a power-law distribution at the top end, and many media platforms limit the number of friends or followers a person can have. For more information about scale-free networks, see Barabasi (2003). For a brief discussion on the measurement and analysis of online social networks, see Mislove et al. (2007).

4 Note that a network can have multiple cores, and different kinds of cores. Since we are concerned with the spread of viral events across media platforms, we can think of the core as those people or organizations who are linked together and who link together the larger network. For more information, see Barabasi (2003), Borgatti and Everett (2000), and Wasserman and Faust (1994).

5 For a co-linking analysis of the viral video and blog data, see Nahon and Hemsley (2011). Also see Karpf (2008) for an index of top political blogs.

6 See Watts (2004) for an excellent discussion. See also Lussier and Chawla (2011) for a recent empirical study on Twitter.
7 For a few studies on how attention for content decays over time, see Wu and Huberman (2007), Crane and Sornette (2008), and Asur et al. (2011).

Chapter 6: Networked Changed Societies

1 https://www.youtube.com/watch?v=owGykVbfgUE
2 http://www.ted.com/pages/great_moments_in_tedtalks
3 To find out if the growth was the result of social sharing, we contacted Daphne Koller, a researcher at Stanford University and one of the co-founders of Coursera, and asked if they could analyze their website referral traffic data to find out where visitors were coming from. A whopping 40 percent of first-time visitors arrived at their site from Facebook, with Gmail at 7 percent and Twitter coming in at 4 percent. Interestingly, Daphne Koller's analysis also shows that even when looking at total traffic, not just first time, all of the top 10 referral locations except one are from what could be considered social media: Facebook, Twitter, Reddit, Facebook Mobile, Gmail, Y!Mail, Class-central (blog), Habrahabr (blog) and Coursera. We should stress that while there is great interest in massive open online courses (MOOCs) and their potential, the media has tended to focus more on the large enrolment numbers and less on the competition rates, which *The New York Times* reported at roughly 5 percent (http://www.nytimes.com/2012/11/20/education/colleges-turn-to-crowd-sourcing-courses.html). This doesn't detract from the value of these courses, but highlights that virality can spread even when exact information is limited or missing. In terms

of speed, we note that within just a year, Coursera has grown enough that it offers about 157 courses with over 2 million students, from across more than 196 countries (email interview with Daphne Koller, Coursera founder, December 6, 2012).

4 See MediaMatter For America's Blog for a detailed timeline of the event: http://mediamatters.org/research/2010/07/22/timeline-of-breitbarts-sherrod-smear/168090

5 Bourdieu believed that actions create and reproduce the social structure in which the actions are embedded. However, he conceptualized habitus happening mainly as a result of a non-intentional and non-conscious internalized structure, rather than conscious intentions to reproduce the social structure (as Anthony Giddens contemplated).

6 http://www.youtube.com/user/officialpsy

7 More specifically, *systems* are the organized relationships between actors (individuals or collectives). *Structures* are the rules and resources organized as properties of a social system. *Structuration* is the collection of "conditions governing the continuity or transmutation of structures, and therefore the reproduction of social systems" (Giddens 1986: 25). Thus, while structures and systems are perceived as temporally continuous, they are actually evolving and mutating under a process of structuration.

8 Schedler and Plattner define accountability as "A is accountable to B when A is obliged to inform B about A's (past or future) actions and decisions, to justify them, and to suffer punishment in the case of eventual misconduct" (1999: 17). See also Anita Allen's critical view of personal accountability (2003).

9 We refer to the broader sense of transparency, the obligation to inform and make data and information accessible to people in a manner that allows it to be used in a variety of ways (including processing or improving it).

10 The open government partnership is a coalition of 55 states that agreed to adopt the principles of open government. See http://www.opengovpartnership.org/open-government-declaration

11 WikiLeaks is an international nonprofit organization, founded in 2006 by Julian Assange, which publishes secret and classified information, and news leaks.

12 http://www.guardian.co.uk/news/datablog/2010/nov/29/wikileaks-cables-data

13 Yochai Benkler (2011) studied the WikiLeaks U.S. embassy cables in depth.

14 http://www.guardian.co.uk/world/interactive/2010/nov/28/us-embassy-cables-wikileaks

15 An interview with Simon Rogers, editor of the datablog and datastore, in *The Guardian*, October 12, 2012.

16 See, for example, the memorandum for the heads of executive departments and agencies issued on January 2011. http://www.whitehouse.gov/sites/default/files/omb/memoranda/2011/m11-08.pdf

Chapter 7: Afterlife

1 And indeed, that message was well internalized as it spread like wildfire within, as well as beyond, its target audience. In a survey, the Pew Research Center found that individuals between the ages of 18 and 29 were much more likely than older adults to watch the video and find out about it through social media (Pew Research Center 2012a). Gilad Lotan conducted a network analysis of the Twitter information flow related to the video and found that the main reason this video went viral was the many pre-existing networks of youth that the Invisible Children organization had been cultivating for years (Lotan 2012).

Danah boyd claims that "most of how they've gotten the message out is by engaging youth" (boyd 2012), actively encouraging them to share the video with a preset list of celebrities (20 culture-makers and 12 policymakers to be exact), and to urge them to call for action against Kony. Thus, two sets of gatekeepers were involved in the diffusion of the video: youth and celebrities.

2 Note that while we are talking about *a* society, it is important to note that viral events can span groups, communities, and societies.

References

ACLU (American Civil Liberties Union). 2012. "UC Davis Students Reach $1 Million Settlement with University Over Pepper-Spraying Incident." September 26. http://www.aclu.org/print/free-speech/uc-davis-students-reach-1-million-settlement-university-over-pepper-spraying-incident

Allen, A. 2003. *Why Privacy Isn't Everything: Feminist Reflections on Personal Accountability*. Lanham, MD: Rowman & Littlefield.

Allsop, D. T., B. R. Bassett, and J. A. Hoskins. 2007. "Word-of-Mouth Research: Principles and Applications." *Journal of Advertising Research* 47 (4): 398–411.

Ancu, M. 2010. "Viral Politics: The Credibility and Effects of Online Viral Political Messages." In M. McKinney and M. Banwart (eds) *Communication in the 2008 U.S. Election: Digital Natives Elect a President*. New York: Peter Lang.

Aral, S. and D. Walker. 2011. "Creating Social Contagion Through Viral Product Design: A Randomized Trial of Peer Influence in Networks." *Management Science* 57 (9): 1623–39.

Aral, S. and D. Walker. 2012. "Identifying Influential and

Susceptible Members of Social Networks." *Science* 337 (6092): 337–41.

Aral, S., L. Muchnik, and A. Sundararajan. 2009. "Distinguishing Influence-based Contagion from Homophily-driven Diffusion in Dynamic Networks." *Proceedings of the National Academy of Sciences* 106 (51): 21544.

Arneson, P. 2006. "Plant Disease Epidemiology: Temporal Aspects." *The Plant Health Instructor*. Available at: https://www.apsnet.org/edcenter/advanced/topics/EpidemiologyTemporal/Pages/default.aspx

Asur, S., B. A. Huberman, G. Szabo, and C. Wang. 2011. "Trends in Social Media: Persistence and Decay." In *5th International AAAI Conference on Weblogs and Social Media*. Barcelona, July 17–21.

Bakshy, E., J. M. Hofman, W. A. Mason, and D. J. Watts. 2011. "Everyone's an Influencer: Quantifying Influence on Twitter." In *Proceedings of the Fourth ACM International Conference on Web Search and Data Mining*. New York: ACM, pp. 65–74.

Bakshy, E., I. Rosenn, C. Marlow, and L. Adamic. 2012. "The Role of Social Networks in Information Diffusion." In *WWW '12: Proceedings of the 21st International Conference on World Wide Web*. New York: ACM, pp. 519–28.

Bampo, M., M. T. Ewing, D. R. Mather, D. Stewart, and M. Wallace. 2008. "The Effects of the Social Structure of Digital Networks on Viral Marketing Performance." *Information Systems Research* 19 (3): 273–90.

Bandura, A. 1989. "Social Cognitive Theory." *Annals of Child Development* 6: 1–60.

Barabasi, A. L. 2003. *Linked*. New York: Plume.

Barash, V., C. Cameron, and M. Macy. 2012. "Critical Phenomena in Complex Contagions." *Social Networks* 34 (4): 451–61.

Barzilai-Nahon, K. 2008. "Toward a Theory of Network Gatekeeping: A Framework for Exploring Information Control." *Journal of the American Society for Information Science and Technology* 59: 1493–512.

Barzilai-Nahon, K. 2009. "Gatekeeping: A Critical Review." *Annual Review of Information Science and Technology* 43: 433–78.

Barzilai-Nahon, K. and R. M. Mason. 2010. "How Executives Perceive the Net Generation." *Information, Communication & Society* 13 (3): 396–418.

Benkler, Y. 2006. *The Wealth of Networks: How Social Production Transforms Markets and Freedom*. New Haven, CT: Yale University Press.

Benkler, Y. 2011. "A Free Irresponsible Press: Wikileaks and the Battle Over the Soul of the Networked Fourth Estate." *Harvard Civil Rights-Civil Liberties Law Review* 46: 311–97.

Bertot, J. C., P. T. Jaeger, and J. M. Grimes. 2012. "Promoting Transparency and Accountability through ICTs, Social Media, and Collaborative E-government." *Transforming Government: People, Process and Policy* 6 (1): 78–91.

Bikhchandani, S., D. Hirshleifer, and I. Welch. 1992. "A Theory of Fads, Fashion, Custom, and Cultural Change as Informational Cascades." *Journal of Political Economy* 100 (5): 992–1026.

Birchler, U. W. and M. Bütler. 2007. *Information Economics*. New York: Routledge.

Bisgin, H., N. Agarwal, and X. Xu. 2010. "Investigating Homophily in Online Social Networks." In *2010 IEEE/WIC/ACM International Conference on Web Intelligence and Intelligent Agent Technology (WI-IAT)*. New York: IEEE, pp. 533–6.

Blankenship, M. 2009. "Two Reasons Susan Boyle Means So Much to Us". Blog. Huffington Post, April 16. Available at:

References

http://www.huffingtonpost.com/mark-blankenship/two-reasons-susan-boyle-m_b_187901.html

Borgatti, S. P. and M. G. Everett. 2000. "Models of Core/periphery Structures." *Social Networks* 21 (4): 375–95.

Boster, F. J., M. R. Kotowski, K. R. Andrews, and K. Serota. 2011. "Identifying Influence: Development and Validation of the Connectivity, Persuasiveness, and Maven Scales." *Journal of Communication* 61 (1): 178–96.

Bourdieu, P. 1977. *Outline of a Theory of Practice* (trans. R. Nice). Cambridge: Cambridge University Press.

Bourdieu, P. 1984. *Distinction: A Social Critique of the Judgement of Taste*. Cambridge, MA: Harvard University Press.

Bourdieu, P. 1990. *The Logic of Practice*. Stanford, CA: Stanford University Press.

boyd, d. m. 2008. *Taken Out of Context: American Teen Sociality in Networked Publics*. Ann Arbor, MI: ProQuest.

boyd, d. 2012. "The Power of Youth: How Invisible Children Orchestrated Kony 2012." Huffington Post, March 14. Available at: http://www.huffingtonpost.com/danah-boyd/post_3126_b_1345782.html

boyd, d., S. Golder, and G. Lotan. 2010. "Tweet, Tweet, Retweet: Conversational Aspects of Retweeting on Twitter." In *2010 43rd Hawaii International Conference on System Sciences (HICSS)*, 1–10. doi:10.1109/HICSS.2010.412.

Boynton, R. 2009. "Going Viral: The Dynamics of Attention." In *Conference Proceedings YouTube and the 2008 Election Cycle*. Amherst, MA: ScholarWorks@UMass Amherst, pp. 11–38.

Braman, S. 2009. *Change of State: Information, Policy, and Power*. Cambridge, MA: The MIT Press.

Brown, J. J. and P. H. Reingen. 1987. "Social Ties and Word-of-Mouth Referral Behavior." *The Journal of Consumer Research* 14 (3): 350–62.

159

References

Broxton, T., Y. Interian, J. Vaver, and M. Wattenhofer. 2010. "Catching a Viral Video." In *International Conference On Data Mining Workshops*. Los Alamitos, CA: IEEE Computer Society, pp. 296–304. Available at: http://static. googleusercontent.com/external_content/untrusted_dlcp/ research.google.com/en/us/pubs/archive/36697.pdf

Burgess, J. and J. Green. 2009. *YouTube: Online Video and Participatory Culture*. Cambridge: Polity.

Burt, R. S. 2004. "Structural Holes and Good Ideas." *American Journal of Sociology* 110 (2): 349–99.

Castells, M. 2009. *Communication Power*. Oxford: Oxford University Press.

Castells, M. 2012. *Networks of Outrage and Hope: Social Movements in the Internet Age*. Cambridge: Polity.

Centola, D. and M. Macy. 2005. "Complex Contagion and the Weakness of Long Ties." *American Journal of Sociology* 113 (3): 702–34.

Christakis, N. A. and J. H. Fowler. 2009. *Connected: The Surprising Power of Our Social Networks and How They Shape Our Lives*. New York: Little, Brown and Company.

Clauset, A., C. R. Shalizi, and M. E. J. Newman. 2009. "Power-Law Distributions in Empirical Data." *SIAM Review* 51 (4): 661–703.

Crane, R. and D. Sornette. 2008. "Robust Dynamic Classes Revealed by Measuring the Response Function of a Social System." *Proceedings of the National Academy of Sciences* 105 (41): 15649–53.

De Bruyn, A. and G. L. Lilien 2008. "A Multi-stage Model of Word-of-Mouth Influence through Viral Marketing." *International Journal of Research in Marketing* 25 (3): 151–63.

Deschâtres, F. and D. Sornette. 2005. "Dynamics of Book Sales: Endogenous Versus Exogenous Shocks in Complex Networks." *Physical Review E* 72 (1): 016112.

References

DFA (Davis Faculty Association). 2011. "DFA Board Calls for Katehi's Resignation." November 19. Available at: http://ucdfa.org/2011/11/dfa-board-calls-for-katehis-resig nation/

Dicker, R., F. Coronado, D. Koo, and R. G. Parrish. 2006. *Principles of Epidemiology in Public Health Practice*, 3rd edn. Atlanta, GA: U.S. Department of Health and Human Services. Centers for Disease Control and Prevention (CDC).

Dobele, A., D. Toleman, and M. Beverland. 2005. "Controlled Infection! Spreading the Brand Message through Viral Marketing." *Business Horizons* 48 (2): 143–9.

Dove, R. 1999. "The Torchbearer ROSA PARKS." *Time*, June 14. Available at: http://www.time.com/time/maga zine/article/0,9171,991252,00.html

Drezner, D. and H. Farrell. 2008. "The Power and Politics of Blogs." *Public Choice* 134 (1–2): 15–30.

Durkheim, E. 1982. *Rules of Sociological Method*. New York: Free Press.

Ellison, N. B., C. Lampe, C. Steinfield, and J. Vitak. 2010. "With a Little Help From My Friends: How Social Network Sites Affect Social Capital Processes." In Z. Papacharissi, (ed.) *A Networked Self: Identity, Community, and Culture on Social Network Sites*. New York: Routledge, pp. 124–45.

Ferguson, R. 2008. "Word of Mouth and Viral Marketing: Taking the Temperature of the Hottest Trends in Marketing." *Journal of Consumer Marketing* 25 (3): 179–82.

Fisher, M. 2012. "Gangnam Style, Dissected: The Subversive Message within South Korea's Music Video Sensation." *The Atlantic*, August 23. Available at: http:// www.theatlantic.com/international/archive/2012/08/ gangnam-style-dissected-the-subversive-message-within-south-koreas-music-video-sensation/261462/

Foucault, M. 1978. *Discipline & Punish: The Birth of the Prison*. 2nd edn. New York: Vintage.

Foucault, M. 1990. *The History of Sexuality* (trans. R. Hurley). New York: Vintage.

Galloway, A. R. 2004. *Protocol: How Control Exists after Decentralization*. Cambridge, MA: The MIT Press.

Giddens, A. 1986. *The Constitution of Society: Outline of the Theory of Structuration*. Berkeley, CA: University of California Press.

Gladwell, M. 2002. *The Tipping Point: How Little Things Can Make a Big Difference*. New York: Back Bay Books.

Goffman, E. 1990. *The Presentation of Self in Everyday Life*. New York: Penguin Books.

Golan, G. J. and L. Zaidner. 2008. "Creative Strategies in Viral Advertising: An Application of Taylor's Six-Segment Message Strategy Wheel." *Journal of Computer-Mediated Communication* 13 (4): 959–72.

González-Bailón, S., J. Borge-Holthoefer, A. Rivero, and Y. Moreno. 2011. "The Dynamics of Protest Recruitment Through an Online Network." *Scientific Reports* 1, article 197.

Goodreau, S. M., J. A. Kitts, and M. Morris. 2009. "Birds of a Feather, or Friend of a Friend? Using Exponential Random Graph Models to Investigate Adolescent Social Networks." *Demography* 46 (1): 103–25.

Granovetter, M. 1973. "The Strength of Weak Ties." *American Journal of Sociology* 78 (6): 1360–80.

Granovetter, M. 1983. "The Strength of Weak Ties: A Network Theory Revisited." *Sociological Theory* 1: 201–33.

Harvard Business Review. 2012. "United Breaks Guitars." Available at: http://hbr.org/product/united-breaks-guitars/an/510057-PDF-ENG

References

Helm, S. 2000. "Viral Marketing – Establishing Customer Relationships by 'Word-of-Mouse.'" *Electronic Markets* 10 (3): 158–61.

Hemsley, J. and R. M. Mason. 2012. "Knowledge and Knowledge Management in the Social Media Age." *Journal of Organizational Computing and Electronic Commerce* 23 (1–2): 138–67.

Herrema, R. 2011. "Flickr, Communities of Practice and the Boundaries of Identity: A Musician Goes Visual." *Visual Studies* 26 (2): 135–41.

Holocomb, J. 2011. "Osama Bin Laden's Death Continues to Dominate the News." *PEJ News Coverage Index: May 2–8, 2011*, May. Available at: http://www.journalism.org/index_report/pej_news_coverage_index_may_2_8_2011.

Hovland, C. I. and W. Weiss. 1951. "The Influence of Source Credibility on Communication Effectiveness." *The Public Opinion Quarterly* 15 (4): 635–50.

Hu, M., S. Liu, F. Wei, Y. Wu, J. Stasko, and K.-L. Ma. 2012. "Breaking News on Twitter." In *Proceedings of the 2012 ACM Annual Conference on Human Factors in Computing Systems*, 2751–4. CHI '12. New York: ACM.

Huberman, B. and L. Adamic. 2004. "Information Dynamics in the Networked World." *Lecture Notes in Physics* 650: 371–98.

International Criminal Court. 2005. "ICC – Warrant of Arrest Unsealed against Five LRA Commanders." Available at: http://www.icc-cpi.int/en_menus/icc/situa tions%20and%20cases/situations/situation%20icc%20 0204/related%20cases/icc%200204%200105/press%20 releases/Pages/warrant%20of%20arrest%20unsealed%20 against%20five%20lra%20commanders.aspx

Jenkins, H. 2009. "If It Doesn't Spread, It's Dead (Part Two): Sticky and Spreadable – Two Paradigms." *Confessions of an Aca-Fan – The Official Weblog of Henry Jenkins,*

February 13. Available at: http://henryjenkins.org/2009/02/ if_it_doesnt_spread_its_dead_p_1.html

Jones, B. D. 1999. "Bounded Rationality." *Annual Review of Political Science* 2 (1): 297–321.

Jurvetson, S., 2000. From the Ground Floor: What Exactly Is Viral Marketing? *Red Herring Communications*, May, pp. 110–11.

Jurvetson, S. and T. Draper. 1997. "Viral Marketing: Viral Marketing Phenomenon Explained." Available at: http://www.dfj.com/news/article_26.shtml

Kahneman, D. 2003. "Maps of Bounded Rationality: Psychology for Behavioral Economics." *American Economic Review* 93 (5): 1449–75.

Kahneman, D. 2010. *The Riddle of Experience vs. Memory.* TED. Available at: http://www.ted.com/talks/daniel_kah neman_the_riddle_of_experience_vs_memory.html.

Kahneman, D., B. Fredrickson, C. Schreiber, and D. Redelmeier. 1993. "When More Pain Is Preferred to Less: Adding a Better End." *Psychological Science* 4 (6): 401–5.

Karpf, D. 2008. Measuring Influence in the Political Blogosphere: Who Is Winning and How Can We Tell? *Politics and Technology Review*: 33–41. Available at: http://www.the4dgroup.com/BAI/articles/PoliTechArticle. pdf

Katz, E. and P. Lazarsfeld. 1955. *Personal Influence: The Part Played by People in the Flow of Mass Communications.* Piscataway, NJ: Transaction Publishers.

Kirby, J. and P. Marsden. 2012. *Connected Marketing.* London: Routledge.

Kiss, C. and M. Bichler. 2008. "Identification of Influencers – Measuring Influence in Customer Networks." *Decision Support Systems* 46 (1): 233–53.

Kitsak, M., L. K. Gallos, S. Havlin, F. Liljeros, L. Muchnik, H. E. Stanley, and H. A. Makse. 2010. "Identifying

Influential Spreaders in Complex Networks." *Nature Physics* 6: 888–93.

Knobel, M. and C. Lankshear. 2007. "Online Memes, Affinities, and Cultural Production." In M. Knobel and C. Lankshear (eds) *A New Literacies Sampler*. New York: Peter Lang.

Kozinets, R. V., K. De Valck, A. C. Wojnicki, and S. J. S. Wilner. 2010. "Networked Narratives: Understanding Word-of-Mouth Marketing in Online Communities." *Journal of Marketing* 74 (2): 71–89.

Krishnamurthy, S. 2001. "Understanding Online Message Dissemination: Analyzing 'Send a Message to a Friend' Data." *First Monday* 6 (5). Available at: http://www.first-monday.org/ojs/index.php/fm/article/view/856

Kwak, H., C. Lee, H. Park, and S. Moon. 2010. "What Is Twitter, a Social Network or a News Media?" In *Proceedings of the 19th International Conference on World Wide Web*, 591–600. New York: ACM.

Lauw, H. W., J. C. Shafer, R. Agrawal, and A. Ntoulas. 2010. "Homophily in the Digital World." *IEEE Internet Computing* 14 (2): 15–23.

Leskovec, J., A. Singh, and J. Kleinberg. 2006. "Patterns of Influence in a Recommendation Network." *Proceedings of the 10th Pacific-Asia Conference on Advances in Knowledge Discovery and Data Mining*: 380–9.

Leskovec, J., L. A. Adamic, and B. A. Huberman. 2007a. "The Dynamics of Viral Marketing." *ACM Transactions on the Web (TWEB)* 1 (1): article 5.

Leskovec, J., M. McGlohon, C. Faloutsos, N. Glance, and M. Hurst. 2007b. "Cascading Behavior in Large Blog Graphs." *Arxiv Preprint arXiv:0704.2803*.

Leskovec, J., L. Backstrom, and J. Kleinberg. 2009. "Meme-tracking and the Dynamics of the News Cycle." In *Proceedings of the 15th ACM SIGKDD International*

Conference on Knowledge Discovery and Data Mining, 497–506. KDD '09. New York: ACM.

Lotan, G. 2012. "[Data Viz] KONY2012: See How Invisible Networks Helped a Campaign Capture the World's Attention." SocialFlow Blog, March 14. Available at: http:// blog.socialflow.com/post/7120244932/data-viz-kony 2012-see-how-invisible-networks-helped-a-campaign-cap ture-the-worlds-attention.

Lotan, G. and D. Gaffney. 2011. "Breaking Bin Laden: Visualizing the Power of a Single Tweet". Blog. *SocialFlow Blog*, May 6. Available at: http://blog.socialflow.com/ post/5246404319/breaking-bin-laden-visualizing-the-power-of-a-single.

Louch, H. 2000. "Personal Network Integration: Transitivity and Homophily in Strong-tie Relations." *Social Networks* 22 (1): 45–64.

Lukes, S. 2005. *Power: A Radical View*, 2nd edn. Basingstoke: Palgrave Macmillan.

Lussier, J. and N. Chawla. 2011. "Network Effects on Tweeting." In T. Elomaa, J. Hollmén and H. Mannila (eds) *Discovery Science*. New York: Springer, pp. 209–20.

Mahajan, V. and R. A. Peterson. 1985. *Models for Innovation Diffusion*. Newbury Park, CA: Sage Publications.

Mayer-Schönberger, V. 2009. *Delete: The Virtue of Forgetting in the Digital Age*. Princeton, NJ: Princeton University Press.

McDermott, P., A. Bennett, and A. Paulson. 2011. *2011 Secrecy Report*. OpenTheGovernment.org. Available at: http://www.openthegovernment.org/sites/default/files/ SRC_2011.pdf.

McPherson, M., L. Smith-Lovin, and J. M. Cook. 2001. "Birds of a Feather: Homophily in Social Networks." *Annual Review of Sociology* 27: 415–44.

Medina, J. 2009. *Brain Rules: 12 Principles for Surviving and*

Thriving at Work, Home, and School. Seattle, WA: Pear Press.

Metoyer-Duran, C. 1991. "Information-Seeking Behavior of Gatekeepers in Ethnolinguistic Communities: Overview of a Taxonomy." *Library and Information Science Research* 13 (4): 319–46.

Metoyer-Duran, C. 1993. "Information Gatekeepers." *Annual Review of Information Science and Technology* 28: 111–50.

Miron-Shatz, T., A. Stone, and D. Kahneman. 2009. "Memories of Yesterday's Emotions: Does the Valence of Experience Affect the Memory-Experience Gap?" *Emotion* 9 (6): 885–91.

Mislove, A., M. Marcon, K. P. Gummadi, P. Druschel, and B. Bhattacharjee. 2007. "Measurement and Analysis of Online Social Networks." In *IMC'07. Proceedings of the 7th ACM SIGCOMM Conference on Internet Measurement*. New York: ACM, pp. 29–42.

Nahapiet, J. and S. Ghoshal. 1998. "Social Capital, Intellectual Capital, and the Organizational Advantage." *The Academy of Management Review* 23 (2): 242–66.

Nahon, K. 2011. "Fuzziness of Inclusion/Exclusion in Networks." *International Journal of Communication* 5: 756–72.

Nahon, K. and J. Hemsley. 2011. "Democracy.com: A Tale of Political Blogs and Content." In *HICSS-44. Proceedings of the 44th Hawaii International Conference on System Sciences*. New York: IEEE.

Nahon, K., J. Hemsley, S. Walker, and M. Hussain. 2011. "Fifteen Minutes of Fame: The Place of Blogs in the Life Cycle of Viral Political Information." *Policy & Internet* 3 (1): 1–28.

Nahon, K., J. Hemsley, R. Mason, S. Walker, and J. Eckert. 2013. "Information Flows in Events of Political Unrest." In *iConference 2013 Proceedings*, pp. 480–5.

Obama, B. 2009. "Transparency and Open Government." The White House, May. Available at: http://www.whitehouse.gov/the_press_office/TransparencyandOpenGovernment

O'Neil, M. 2011. "Death Threats Persuade Alexandra Wallace To Leave UCLA." Blog. *SocialTimes.com*, March 21. Available at: http://socialtimes.com/death-threats-persuade-alexandra-wallace-to-leave-ucla_b42663

Onsemiro. 2012. "Korean Music: PSY's 'Gangnam Style' and 'Gangnam Oppa' in 'Architecture 101' (1)." *My Dear Korea*. Available at: http://mydearkorea.blogspot.com/2012/08/korean-music-psys-gangnam-style-and.html

Palka, W., K. Pousttchi, and D. G. Wiedemann. 2009. "Mobile Word-of-Mouth – A Grounded Theory of Mobile Viral Marketing." *Journal of Information Technology* 24 (2): 172–85.

Parks, R. and J. Haskins. 1999. *Rosa Parks: My Story*. New York: Puffin.

Pastor-Satorras, R. and A. Vespignani. 2001. "Epidemic Spreading in Scale-free Networks." *Physical Review Letters* 86 (14): 3200–3.

Petrovic, S., M. Osborne, and V. Lavrenko. 2011. "RT to Win! Predicting Message Propagation in Twitter." In *Fifth International AAAI Conference on Weblogs and Social Media*. http://www.aaai.org/ocs/index.php/ICWSM/ICWSM11/paper/viewPaper/2754

Pew Research Center. 2012a. *The Viral Kony 2012 Video*. Pew Internet & American Life Project. Available at: http://pewinternet.org/Reports/2012/Kony-2012-Video/Main-report.aspx

Pew Research Center. 2012b. "Further Decline in Credibility Ratings for Most News Organizations." *Pew Research Center for the People and the Press*, August 16. Available at: http://www.people-press.org/2012/08/16/further-decline-in-credibility-ratings-for-most-news-organizations/

References

Phelps, J., R. Lewis, L. Mobilio, D. Perry, and N. Raman. 2004. "Viral Marketing or Electronic Word-of-Mouth Advertising: Examining Consumer Responses and Motivations to Pass along Email." *Journal of Advertising Research* 44 (4): 333–48.

Piotrowski, S. J. 2007. *Governmental Transparency in the Path of Adminstrative Reform*. New York: SUNY Press.

Pogrebin, L. C. 2009. "Why Susan Boyle Makes Us Cry." Blog. Huffington Post, April 16. Available at: http://www.huffingtonpost.com/letty-cottin-pogrebin/why-susan-boyle-makes-us_b_187790.html.

Qiu, L., H. Lin, and A. K.-Y. Leung. 2013. "Cultural Differences and Switching of In-Group Sharing Behavior Between an American (Facebook) and a Chinese (Renren) Social Networking Site." *Journal of Cross-Cultural Psychology* 44 (1): 106–21.

Ravikant, N. and A. Rifkin. 2010. "Why Twitter Is Massively Undervalued Compared to Facebook." TechCrunch, October 16. Available at: http://techcrunch.com/2010/10/16/why-twitter-is-massively-undervalued-compared-to-facebook/

Redelmeier, D. A. and D. Kahneman. 1996. "Patients' Memories of Painful Medical Treatments: Real-time and Retrospective Evaluations of Two Minimally Invasive Procedures." *Pain* 66 (1): 3–8.

Redelmeier, D. A., J. Katz, and D. Kahneman. 2003. "Memories of Colonoscopy: A Randomized Trial." *Pain* 104 (1–2): 187–94.

Relly, J. and M. Sabharwal. 2009. "Perceptions of Transparency of Government Policymaking: A Cross-national Study." *Government Information Quarterly* 26 (1): 148–57.

Roberts, A. 2006. *Blacked Out: Government Secrecy in the Information Age*. Cambridge: Cambridge University Press.

References

Rogers, E. M. 2003. *Diffusion of Innovations*, 5th edn. New York: Free Press.

Sagolla, D. 2009. *140 Characters*. Hoboken, NJ: John Wiley & Sons.

Schedler, A. and M. Plattner. 1999. *The Self Restraining State: Power and Accountability in New Democracies*. Boulder, CO: Lynne Rienner Publishers.

Scheufele, D. A. and D. Tewksbury. 2007. "Framing, Agenda Setting, and Priming: The Evolution of Three Media Effects Models." *Journal of Communication* 57 (1): 9–20.

Schmidt, J. 2007. "Blogging Practices: An Analytical Framework." *Journal of Computer Mediated Communication* 12 (4): 1409–27.

Scott, J. 2011. "UC Davis Pepper Spray Video Explodes Online – YouTube Killed The Evening News." ReelSEO. Available at: http://www.reelseo.com/uc-davis-pepper-spray-video/

Segev, E., N. Ahituv, and K. Nahon. 2007. "Mapping Diversities and Tracing Trends of Cultural Homogeneity/Heterogeneity in Cyberspace." *Journal of Computer Mediated Communication* 12 (4): article 7.

Shalizi, C. R. and A. C. Thomas. 2011. "Homophily and Contagion are Generically Confounded in Observational Social Network Studies." *Sociological Methods & Research* 40 (2): 211–39.

Shifman, L. 2012. "An Anatomy of a YouTube Meme." *New Media & Society* 14 (2): 187–203.

Shifman, L. 2013. "Memes in a Digital World: Reconciling with a Conceptual Troublemaker." *Journal of Computer Mediated Communication* 18 (3): 362–77.

Shifman, L. and M. Blondheim. 2010. "The Medium Is the Joke: Online Humor about and by Networked Computers." *New Media & Society* 12 (8): 1348–67.

Shirky, C. 2009. *Here Comes Everybody: The Power of*

Organizing Without Organizations. Harmondsworth: Penguin.

Simon, H. A. 1955. "A Behavioral Model of Rational Choice." *The Quarterly Journal of Economics* 69 (1): 99–118.

Smith, A. 2009. *The Internet's Role in Campaign 2008*. Pew Internet & American Life Project. Available at: http://www.pewinternet.org/Reports/2009/6--The-Internets-Role-in-Campaign-2008/1--Summary-of-Findings.aspx

Stanton, S. 2012. "Officer at Center of Pepper-Spraying Incident No Longer Works at UC Davis." August 1. http://www.sacbee.com/2012/08/01/v-print/4679893/officer-at-center-of-pepper-spraying.html.

Stelter, B. 2010. "When Race Is the Issue, Misleading Coverage Sets Off an Uproar." *The New York Times*, July 26. Available at: http://www.nytimes.com/2010/07/26/business/media/26race.html?_r=1.

Suh, B., L. Hong, P. Pirolli, and E. H Chi. 2010. "Want to Be Retweeted? Large Scale Analytics on Factors Impacting Retweet in Twitter Network." In *Social Computing (SocialCom), 2010 IEEE Second International Conference On*, 177–84. New York: IEEE.

Sunstein, C. 2001. *Republic.com*. Princeton, NJ: Princeton University Press.

Swartz, D. 1997. *Culture & Power: The Sociology of Pierre Bourdieu*. Chicago, IL: University of Chicago Press.

Taleb, N. N. 2010. *The Black Swan: The Impact of the Highly Improbable*, 2nd edn. New York: Random House.

"TED: Ideas Worth Spreading." 2012. Available at: http://www.ted.com/

Thompson, J. B. 1984. *Studies in the Theory of Ideology*. Berkeley, CA: University of California Press.

Thorngate, W. 1988. "On Paying Attention." In W. Baker, L. Mos, H. Rappard, and H. Stam (eds) *Recent Trends in Theoretical Psychology: Proceedings of the Second Biannual Conference of the International Society for Theoretical Psychology, April 10–25, 1987, Banff, Alberta, Canada.* Berlin: Springer-Verlag, 247–63.

Tushman, M. L. and R. Katz. 1980. "External Communication and Project Performance: An Investigation into the Role of Gatekeepers." *Management Science* 26 (11): 1071–85.

Valente, T. W. 1996. "Network Models of the Diffusion of Innovations." *Computational & Mathematical Organization Theory* 2 (2): 163–4.

Van der Lans, R., G. van Bruggen, J. Eliashberg, and B. Wierenga. 2010. "A Viral Branching Model for Predicting the Spread of Electronic Word of Mouth." *Marketing Science* 29 (2): 348–65.

Vasalou, A., A. N. Joinson, and D. Courvoisier. 2010. "Cultural Differences, Experience with Social Networks and the Nature of 'True Commitment' in Facebook." *International Journal of Human-Computer Studies* 68 (10): 719–28.

Wallsten, K. 2010. "'Yes We Can': How Online Viewership, Blog Discussion, Campaign Statements and Mainstream Media Coverage Produced a Viral Video Phenomenon." *Journal of Information Technology & Politics* 7 (2): 163–81.

Wallsten, K. 2011. "Many Sources, One Message: Political Blog Links to Online Videos during the 2008 Campaign." *Journal of Political Marketing* 10 (1): 88–114.

Walther, J. B., C. T. Carr, S. S. W. Choi, D. C. DeAndrea, J. Kim, S. T. Tong, and B. Van der Heide. 2010. "Interaction of Interpersonal, Peer, and Media Influence Sources Online." In Z. Papacharissi (ed.) *A Networked Self: Identity, Community, and Culture on Social Network Sites.* New York: Routledge, pp. 17–38.

Wasserman, S. and K. Faust. 1994. *Social Network Analysis:*

Methods and Applications. Cambridge: Cambridge University Press.

Watts, D. J. 2004. *Six Degrees: The Science of a Connected Age.* New York: W. W. Norton.

Watts, D. J. and P. S. Dodds. 2007. "Influentials, Networks, and Public Opinion Formation." *Journal of Consumer Research* 34 (4): 441–58.

Weber, M. 1946. *From Max Weber: Essays in Sociology* (trans. and ed. H. H. Gerth and C. Wright Mills). Oxford: Oxford University Press.

Wenger, E. 1998. *Communities of Practice: Learning, Meaning, and Identity.* Cambridge: Cambridge University Press.

Wilkerson, M. 2012. "Joseph Kony Is Not in Uganda (and Other Complicated Things)." *Foreign Policy Blogs.* Available at: http://blog.foreignpolicy.com/posts/2012/03/07/guest_post_joseph_kony_is_not_in_uganda_and_other_complicated_things?wp_login_redirect=0

Wilson, S. 2011. "Alexandra Wallace, UCLA Student, Rants on Asians for Phoning Tsunami Victims in the Library (VIDEO)." *LA Weekly Blogs*, March 14. Available at: http://blogs.laweekly.com/informer/2011/03/alexandra_wallace_ucla_girl_rant_asians_in_the_library.php

Wu, F. and B. A. Huberman. 2007. "Novelty and Collective Attention." *Proceedings of the National Academy of Sciences* 104 (45): 17599–601.

Wu, S., J. M. Hofman, W. A. Mason, and D. J. Watts. 2011. "Who Says What to Whom on Twitter." In *Proceedings of the 20th International Conference on World Wide Web.* New York: ACM, 705–14.

Yang, J. and J. Leskovec. 2010. "Modeling Information Diffusion in Implicit Networks." In *2010 IEEE 10th International Conference on Data Mining (ICDM).* New York: IEEE, 599–608.

References

Zuckerman, E. 2012. "Unpacking Kony 2012." *My Heart's in Accra*. Available at: http://www.ethanzuckerman.com/blog/2012/03/08/unpacking-kony-2012/

Index

Index

Index

Index

Index

Index

Index

Index